Forex Trading Frontier: Navigating Currency Markets for Profit

Mastering Strategies for Successful Forex Trading

Adam Bennett

Table of Contents

INTRODUCTION

The thorough manual "Forex Trading Frontier: Navigating Currency Markets for Profit - Mastering Strategies for Successful Forex Trading" is a valuable resource for traders of all experience levels who are stepping into the exciting realm of forex trading. Its precise and knowledgeable writing reveals the complex workings of the currency markets, providing priceless information and techniques for confidently navigating the environment.

This book gives traders the tools they need to take advantage of market swings and consistently turn a profit, from breaking down the basics of forex trading to learning sophisticated strategies. It explores important subjects like risk management, psychological toughness, technical and fundamental analysis, and technical analysis, promoting a comprehensive grasp of market dynamics.

With years of experience and knowledge, the author simplifies difficult ideas into manageable portions so that traders of all skill levels can understand them. Each chapter provides useful examples, case studies, and practical guidance to help readers become proficient in the art of forex trading.

"Forex Trading Frontier" is an essential tool for anyone looking to increase their income, gain financial independence, or just get into the thrilling world of currency trading. It provides traders with accurate and insightful guidance through all the highs and lows of the forex market.

CHAPTER I

Understanding Forex Trading

What is trading forex?

The foundation of the world financial market is forex trading, which is an acronym for foreign exchange trading. It stands for the decentralized market place where currencies are traded worldwide. With an average daily trading volume of over $6 trillion, it is larger than the total volume of all stock markets combined. Buying and selling currencies with the ultimate aim of profiting from changes in exchange rates is the core of forex trading. Forex, in contrast to traditional stock markets, is open twenty-four hours a day, five days a week, and crosses major financial centers in multiple time zones.

The idea of currency pairs lies at the core of forex trading. All transactions involving the exchange of one currency for another involve the constant trading of currencies in pairs. The most traded currency pairs are GBP/USD (British Pound/US Dollar), EUR/USD (Euro/US Dollar), and USD/JPY (US Dollar/Japanese Yen). Every pair of currencies indicates the rate of exchange between the two, providing insight into their relative values. When the EUR/USD exchange rate is 1.20, for example, one Euro is equivalent to 1.20 US dollars.

A large network of financial institutions, including banks, investment firms, central banks, and individual traders, facilitates the forex market's operations. Electronic over-the-counter (OTC) transactions allow for direct dealings between participants through computer networks, eliminating the need for a centralized exchange. The high liquidity of the forex market is a result of its decentralized structure, which allows traders to enter and exit positions with ease—even in large quantities—without having a noticeable impact on prices.

There are many different ways for investors to make money with forex trading. Its ability to leverage capital, which enables traders to command large positions with relatively small amounts of capital, is notably one of its main advantages. But it's important to recognize that leverage increases gains as well as losses, so careful risk management is required. In addition, the foreign exchange market exhibits exceptional liquidity, as numerous participants trade continuously. Because of this liquidity, traders are able to execute trades at competitive prices with little to no slippage, which increases their potential for profit.

In order to trade foreign exchange, people usually use a broker to act as a middleman between the trader and the market. Brokers provide traders with access to advanced trading platforms so they can manage their positions, place orders, and perform in-depth market analyses. In order to enable traders to make educated decisions, these platforms frequently include a wide range of tools and features, such as technical indicators, real-time news feeds, and sophisticated charting tools.

A number of important players are present in the forex market, and each is essential to its dynamics. In order to stabilize exchange rates or accomplish particular economic goals, central banks formulate monetary policies and intervene in currency markets, exerting considerable influence. The bulk of forex transactions are dominated by commercial banks, which engage in both speculative trading and meeting the needs of their clients. Hedge funds, investment firms, and multinational corporations are also involved in forex trading, attempting to profit from currency fluctuations by employing a variety of strategies, such as hedging and speculation.

With so many different trading styles and strategies available, forex trading can accommodate a wide range of preferences and goals. By carefully examining price charts and utilizing mathematical indicators, technical analysis helps traders spot patterns and trends that will help them forecast future price movements. On the other hand, fundamental analysis concentrates on assessing the economic, political, and social variables—such as interest rates, inflation, and geopolitical developments—that affect the value of currencies. In order to predict market direction, traders can also incorporate sentiment analysis, which measures investor psychology and market sentiment.

It takes a harmonious combination of knowledge, skill, and discipline to trade forex successfully. To stay on top of the game, traders need to make a commitment to lifelong learning about economic indicators, market dynamics, and trading tactics. Since trading entails losses, putting strong risk management procedures in place is equally essential. To protect capital and maintain profitability, this entails putting stop-loss orders in place, diversifying portfolios, and strictly adhering to risk-to-reward ratios.

Finally, forex trading shows itself to be a dynamic and profitable endeavor that provides investors all over the world with unmatched opportunities. Traders with diverse backgrounds and levels of experience are consistently drawn to it due to its exceptional liquidity, ease of use, and potential for profit. Nevertheless, to succeed in forex trading, one must possess unwavering commitment, tolerance, and flexibility to deal with the constantly shifting market conditions. People can navigate the complexity of the currency markets and achieve their financial goals by understanding the fundamentals of forex trading and adopting reliable trading strategies.

Historical Context of Forex Markets

The interesting journey through centuries of economic, political, and technological evolution that has shaped the global financial landscape is provided by the historical context of forex markets. The need to facilitate international trade and commerce can be traced back to ancient civilizations, which is where currency trading first emerged. Early examples of currency exchange can be seen in Mesopotamia, where transactions involving various currencies were recorded on clay tablets. In a similar vein, currency exchange was used by the ancient Greek, Roman, and Egyptian societies to promote trade across large empires. Currency trading became more organized during the Middle Ages and Renaissance as trade routes and civilizations flourished. Money changers and exchange brokers were established in important trading hubs like Venice, Florence, and Amsterdam. These early financial centers served as a springboard for the development of contemporary banking and finance, with organizations such as Florence's Medici Bank playing a key role in easing currency exchange and trade finance.

The demand for currency exchange was further fueled by mercantilist policies and colonial expansion during the 17th and 18th centuries. Due to the massive international trade that European powers engaged in, different currencies circulated throughout different continents. The creation of colonial trading posts and mercantile outposts made it easier for people to transfer goods and money across international borders. The foundation for contemporary monetary systems was also laid during this period by the introduction of paper money and the growth of centralized banking systems.

The gold standard, which guaranteed stability and predictability in exchange rates by pegging currencies to a fixed amount of gold, was adopted in the 19th century. But in the face of fixed exchange rates and economic imbalances, the gold standard proved to be unworkable. Following the system's collapse during World War I, there was a period of unstable currency rates and monetary instability.

A number of initiatives to bring international financial stability back were made during the interwar years, and the Bretton Woods system was finally established in 1944. Major currencies were tied to the US dollar, which was tied to gold at a set exchange rate, under the terms of the Bretton Woods agreement. In the years following World War II, this system offered a foundation for global monetary cooperation and exchange rate stability. However, because of growing liquidity demands and economic pressures, the Bretton Woods system started to fall apart in the 1960s.

The history of forex markets underwent a sea change with the fall of the Bretton Woods system in the early 1970s. Currency trading became more decentralized and driven by the market as fixed exchange rates were abandoned in favor of a floating exchange rate system. As a result, the contemporary forex market developed, which is distinguished by electronic execution, high liquidity, and 24-hour trading. Online trading platforms and electronic communication networks (ECNs) were made possible by the advancement of computer technology and telecommunications, which enabled electronic currency trading.

Technology breakthroughs, capital market liberalization, and deregulation have propelled the forex market's explosive globalization and growth since the 1970s. Online trading platforms have made it easier for people and organizations from all over the world to access the foreign exchange markets and engage in currency trading. With an average daily trading volume of over $6 trillion, the forex market is currently the largest financial market in the world, far exceeding the combined volume of all stock markets worldwide. It plays a crucial role in the operation of the world economy by acting as a conduit for international trade, investment, and economic activity.

To sum up, the historical background of foreign exchange markets bears witness to the ongoing significance of currency trading in promoting global trade and finance. Currency trading has fueled economic growth and globalization since the dawn of civilization and continues to do so today. Navigating the complexity of the modern forex landscape is made easier for traders by having a solid understanding of the historical underpinnings of the forex markets, which offers insightful knowledge about their dynamics and evolution.

Participants in the Foreign Exchange Market

The forex market, which is regarded as the biggest financial market in the world, is distinguished by the wide range of players that participate in it, each of whom is essential to its dynamics and liquidity. Together, these players—which include central banks, institutional investors, and individual traders—contribute to the thriving currency trading ecosystem. To properly navigate the complexities of the forex market and understand the nuances of forex trading, one must have a thorough understanding of the multifaceted nature of these participants.

Central banks, which control a large amount of the forex market through their monetary policies and interventions, are at its center. By modifying interest rates and carrying out currency interventions, central banks seek to maintain economic growth, regulate inflation, and stabilize exchange rates. They are important participants in the dynamics of the forex market because their actions can have significant impacts on currency values.

A significant role in the forex market is played by commercial banks, which handle most currency transactions. These banks cater to the speculative trading interests of their clients as well as their own needs for currency exchange services. Commercial banks are essential for maintaining seamless transaction flows and supplying liquidity to the foreign exchange market because they have access to enormous pools of liquidity. Commercial banks also participate in proprietary trading, utilizing their resources and experience to profit from currency fluctuations.

Significant players in the forex market are institutional investors, which include pension funds, investment firms, and hedge funds. These companies trade currencies for their own account or on behalf of their clients in an effort to profit from currency fluctuations. In order to take advantage of transient price discrepancies in the foreign exchange market, institutional investors frequently utilize complex trading techniques such as algorithmic trading and high-frequency trading. Their significant trading volumes can affect short-term price movements and add to market liquidity.

For the purpose of controlling their exposure to currency risk, multinational companies also actively trade in the foreign exchange market. These businesses trade currencies as a hedge against unfavorable changes in exchange rates that might have an effect on their profitability and global operations. Multinational firms can reduce currency risk and stabilize their cash flows by utilizing derivatives like forwards, options, and futures contracts. Multinational firms may also participate in speculative trading in order to profit from changes in currency values and improve their financial results.

Small-scale investors and individual traders make up a sizable portion of the forex market, known as retail traders. Modern technology and the emergence of online trading platforms have given retail traders unparalleled access to the forex market from the comfort of their homes. Retail currency traders trade for a variety of reasons, such as speculating, generating income, and accumulating wealth. Retail traders contribute to market liquidity and diversity through their collective trading activities, even though they might not have the resources and knowledge of institutional investors.

In order for retail traders to participate in the forex market, brokers are essential. Retail traders are able to execute trades and effectively manage their positions thanks to these intermediaries' access to trading platforms, market data, and execution services. Brokers can function as electronic communication networks (ECNs), matching buy and sell orders from various market participants, or as market makers, offering liquidity by quoting bid and ask prices for currency pairs. In order to access the forex market and successfully negotiate its complexity, retail traders depend on brokers.

Lastly, speculators are a major factor in the short-term price fluctuations that occur in the forex market. Speculators, which include private traders, hedge funds, and proprietary trading companies, buy and sell currencies depending on their predictions of future price movements in an attempt to profit from currency price fluctuations. Speculative trading helps guarantee that prices appropriately reflect market fundamentals and increases liquidity in the forex market. Excessive speculation, however, can also lead to increased volatility and destabilize currency markets, necessitating regulatory action.

Apart from the aforementioned principal players, there exist additional noteworthy contributors to the dynamics of the foreign exchange market. Governments can affect currency markets through fiscal policies like taxation and spending, especially in countries with floating exchange rate regimes. Currency values can be impacted by international organizations such as the World Bank and the International Monetary Fund (IMF), which offer financial assistance to underprivileged nations. The ecosystem surrounding the forex market has also been further enhanced by the emergence of new players brought about by technological advancements, such as social trading networks and high-frequency trading companies.

To sum up, a wide range of players participate in the forex market, which enhances its resilience, efficiency, and liquidity. Every participant in the currency trading market, including institutional investors, retail traders, brokers, speculators, central banks, and commercial banks, has a distinct impact on the dynamics of the market. Making wise trading decisions and navigating the complexities of the forex market require an understanding of these participants' motivations and behaviors.

Basics of Currency Pairs

Gaining an understanding of the fundamentals of currency pairs is essential to comprehending the complexities of the forex market, which is a necessary ability for anyone wishing to trade currencies. In this vast financial landscape, currency pairs—which depict the relationship between two currencies when one is quoted against the other—serve as the main instruments traded. A thorough understanding of currency pair operations is essential for traders to successfully negotiate the intricacies of the foreign exchange market.

A currency pair consists of the base currency and the quote currency at its core. The currency being bought or sold is known as the base currency, which is indicated as the first currency in the pair. The value of the base currency is represented by the quote currency, which is indicated as the second currency. For example, the US dollar (USD) is the quote currency and the euro (EUR) is the base currency in the EUR/USD currency pair. When the EUR/USD exchange rate is 1.20, it means that one euro is worth 1.20 US dollars.

The ask price and the bid price are the two prices that are normally quoted for currency pairs. The price at which the market is willing to purchase the base currency is represented by the bid price, and the price at which the market is willing to sell the base currency is represented by the ask price. The spread, which includes the transaction costs related to trading currency pairs, is the difference between the ask and bid prices.

The three primary categories of currencies are major pairs, minor pairs, and exotic pairs. The most traded and liquid currencies worldwide are found in major currency pairs. Usually, the US dollar is combined with another significant currency, like the euro, Swiss franc, Japanese yen, or British pound. Major currency pairs include USD/CHF, USD/JPY, EUR/USD, and GBP/USD, as examples.

Minor currency pairs, also called cross currency pairs, are sets of two major currencies other than the US dollar that do not include the dollar. Minor currency pairs include GBP/JPY, EUR/AUD, and EUR/GBP, as examples. One major currency and one currency from a developing or smaller economy are included in exotic currency pairs. Comparing these pairs to major and minor pairs, the spreads are wider and the liquidity is lower. USD/TRY (US dollar/Turkish lira), USD/SEK (US dollar/Swedish krona), and EUR/TRY (euro/Turkish lira) are a few examples of exotic currency pairs.

Forex traders must comprehend the dynamics of currency pairs because these factors have a significant impact on their trading choices and tactics. Trading opportunities are identified, future price movements are predicted, and currency pairs are analyzed by traders using a variety of technical and fundamental analysis techniques.

In order to forecast future price movements, technical analysts examine historical price data and make use of chart patterns, technical indicators, and other instruments. To determine possible entry and exit points in the market, traders can employ tools like trend lines, moving averages, and levels of support and resistance.

Fundamental analysis, on the other hand, is concerned with the social, political, and economic aspects of currency values. Interest rates, inflation, GDP growth, geopolitical events, and central bank policies are a few examples of factors that can affect the supply and demand for currencies, which in turn affects exchange rates. To determine the underlying causes influencing currency pair movements, traders examine economic data releases, central bank statements, and geopolitical events.

Additionally, traders need to take into account the unique traits and behaviors that various currency pairs display when engaging in trading. Major currency pairs are often preferred by day traders and scalpers looking to profit from transient price fluctuations because they typically have tighter spreads and higher liquidity. Even though minor currency pairs have lower liquidity and wider spreads than major currency pairs, they can still present trading opportunities for investors looking to gain exposure to particular currency pairs. Wider spreads and reduced liquidity are characteristics of exotic currency pairs, which are typically traded by more seasoned traders who are prepared to take on greater risk in the hopes of earning larger profits.

In summary, an in-depth knowledge of currency pair fundamentals is necessary to fully grasp the forex market and create successful trading strategies. The relationship between two currencies is represented by currency pairs, and the value of one currency in relation to another is indicated by the exchange rate. Technical and fundamental analysts of currency pairs can provide traders with insights into future price movements and help them make well-informed trading decisions. Furthermore, traders can better navigate the complexities of the forex market and improve their trading success by being aware of the distinct traits and behaviors of various currency pair.

CHAPTER II

Fundamentals of Currency Markets

Supply and Demand Dynamics

Understanding the complex dynamics of supply and demand is imperative for all those engaged in financial market analysis, trading, or investment. Any market's pricing of goods and services is determined by these fundamental economic concepts. Supply and demand dynamics are especially important in the forex market because they shape currency pair exchange rates, which in turn affects trading decisions, investment strategies, and market analysis.

Economics' foundational ideas of supply and demand describe how producers and consumers interact in a market. Demand is the amount of an item or service that buyers are willing to purchase at a specific price, whereas supply is the amount of that good or service that producers are willing to offer for sale at that price. The equilibrium price and quantity in a market are determined by the relationship between supply and demand.

Understanding supply and demand dynamics in the forex market is essential to comprehending changes in exchange rates. Numerous factors, such as capital movements, international trade flows, central bank policies, and economic indicators, affect a currency's supply. An increase in interest rates by a nation's central bank, for instance, may draw in foreign capital inflows and boost demand for the currency. On the other hand, a trade deficit—a nation's excess imports over exports—may result in an excess of that nation's currency on the foreign exchange market, which would pressure the country's exchange rate lower.

Conversely, a currency's demand is determined by variables like investor sentiment, inflation rates, political stability, and the likelihood of economic growth. Strong economic fundamentals and stable political environments usually translate into high demand among investors for the currencies of those nations. For example, when a nation has strong economic growth and low inflation, investors might want to buy its currency, which would raise demand and raise its value on the foreign exchange market.

The relationship between a currency pair's supply and demand determines its equilibrium exchange rate. A currency gains value in relation to other currencies in the pair when demand for it exceeds supply. On the other hand, a currency depreciates when there is an excess of it. Exchange rates frequently fluctuate as a result of these shifts in the dynamics of supply and demand, offering traders the chance to make money through currency trading.

To forecast future price movements in the forex market and analyze supply and demand dynamics, traders utilize a range of technical and fundamental analysis techniques. Technical analysis is the process of examining past price data to find trends and possible trading opportunities using chart patterns, technical indicators, and other tools. To determine important price points where supply and demand are likely to collide, a trader might, for instance, employ moving averages or levels of support and resistance.

Contrarily, fundamental analysis concentrates on the economic, political, and social elements—such as interest rates, inflation, GDP growth, geopolitical developments, and central bank policies—that affect the supply and demand for currencies. Trading decisions in the forex market can be well-informed as traders evaluate the fundamental factors influencing supply and demand dynamics by examining economic data releases, central bank decisions, and geopolitical developments.

Furthermore, speculation and market sentiment can have an impact on the dynamics of supply and demand in the forex market. Short-term price fluctuations in currencies can result from traders' perceptions of economic data releases, central bank decisions, and geopolitical events influencing supply and demand. For instance, a central bank's decision to raise interest rates may be viewed by investors as hawkish, which could lead to higher demand for the currency and an increase in value.

In summary, the dynamics of supply and demand are key ideas that influence how much the forex market's prices fluctuate. To make wise trading decisions and take advantage of market opportunities, traders must have a thorough understanding of the variables affecting the supply and demand for currencies. Technical and fundamental analysis methods can be used by traders to examine supply and demand dynamics in order to gain insights into future price movements and create successful trading strategies for navigating the intricacies of the forex market. The dynamics of supply and demand are further shaped by geopolitical events, macroeconomic trends, and market sentiment, making thorough analysis necessary for profitable forex trading.

Factors Affecting Exchange Rates

Exchange rate-influencing factors are a complex combination of social, political, and economic factors that are deeply entwined with the forex market. Together, these many factors affect how much a currency is worth, which affects traders, investors, governments, and corporations in different ways. To navigate the complexities of currency markets with skill, one must have a thorough understanding of these factors.

Interest rates, which are squarely within the jurisdiction of central banks, are one of the main factors influencing changes in exchange rates. Interest rates are tools that these financial authorities use to control inflation, promote economic expansion, and preserve price stability. Interest rate increases usually attract foreign investors who are attracted by the prospect of earning larger returns on their investments. This, in turn, increases demand for the currency and leads to its appreciation. On the other hand, a drop in interest rates could cause investors to pull their money out of the market in search of better returns elsewhere, which would reduce demand for the currency and cause it to weaken.

Due to their ability to shed light on the state and functioning of economies, economic indicators have a considerable influence over exchange rates. GDP growth, employment reports, inflation rates, trade balances, and other data releases are important indicators of market mood. Positive economic news boosts investor confidence and increases the value of a currency; negative news can undermine investor confidence and cause a depreciation. Traders use these indicators to predict future moves by the central bank and assess the strength of the economy, which helps them make trading decisions.

Exchange rates are significantly impacted by the stability of political environments and the occurrence of geopolitical events, which affect investor sentiment and risk tolerance. Countries that exhibit stable political environments and consistent policymaking tend to attract foreign investment, thereby strengthening their currencies. On the other hand, when investors look for stable havens, events like elections, conflicts, political unrest, or geopolitical tensions can cause volatility and cause currencies to depreciate. These incidents highlight how closely political developments and the workings of the currency market are related.

Exchange rate dynamics are significantly influenced by the policies and interventions of central banks. To affect currency values, these institutions employ monetary policy instruments like interest rate changes, quantitative easing, and currency interventions. Buying or selling currencies on the foreign exchange market is known as currency intervention, and it is done to stabilize exchange rates or accomplish particular policy goals. Although these interventions could have short-term effects on exchange rates, their long-term effectiveness depends on a number of variables, such as the state of the economy and market sentiment.

Exchange rates are fundamentally determined by capital flows and trade balances. Demand for the currencies of nations with trade surpluses—those that export more goods and services than they import—usually rises. The reason for this surge in demand is that overseas purchasers require local currency to make transactions easier. On the other hand, countries that are experiencing trade imbalances and depend on foreign capital inflows to counterbalance their trade may experience currency depreciation.

Short-term changes in exchange rates are significantly influenced by investor and market sentiment. The way in which traders interpret economic data releases, central bank decisions, and geopolitical developments shapes their trading decisions and permanently alters currency prices. Because market sentiment can change quickly in response to news and events, currency markets are known for their volatility.

Exchange rates are also shaped by strategies such as carry trades and speculation. Speculators trade currencies in an attempt to capitalize on short-term price changes based on expectations of future changes in the exchange rate. Carry trade strategies leverage interest rate differentials by borrowing money in low-interest currencies and investing it in higher-interest currencies. These actions affect the dynamics of supply and demand in the foreign exchange market, which puts pressure on exchange rates.

Finally, it should be noted that exchange rates are a complex fabric made up of numerous elements, including interest rates, economic indicators, trade balances, political stability, central bank policies, investor sentiment, and speculative activity. To predict changes in exchange rates and make wise trading decisions, participants in the forex market need to have a keen understanding of these variables and how they interact. Furthermore, in order to strengthen competitiveness and stability in the global economy, businesses and policymakers need to carefully take these factors into account when managing currency exposure and developing economic policies.

Economic Indicators and their Impact

Economic indicators offer important insights into many facets of economic activity and are crucial instruments for evaluating the state and performance of economies. These indicators, which cover a wide range of metrics, help businesses, investors, analysts, and policymakers make wise decisions and comprehend the workings of the world economy.

The GDP, which calculates the total value of goods and services produced within a nation's borders over a given time period, usually a quarter or a year, is one of the most widely followed economic indicators. GDP growth rates show how quickly the economy is expanding or contracting; faster growth rates are indicative of a healthy economy, while slower growth rates are indicative of recessions or slowdowns. Since GDP growth measures an economy's total output and ability to create jobs and revenue, it is a crucial indicator of overall economic health.

The percentage of the labor force that is unemployed and actively looking for work is measured by the unemployment rate, which is another important economic indicator. A low unemployment rate typically denotes full employment and plenty of job opportunities, as well as a robust labor market and robust economic conditions. On the other hand, a high unemployment rate can indicate weak job growth, underutilization of labor resources, and economic distress. Data on unemployment offers insights into the state of the labor market, consumer confidence, and general state of the economy.

The rate of increase in the cost of goods and services over time is reflected in inflation, which is quantified by indices like the Producer Price Index (PPI) and the Consumer Price Index (CPI). A healthy economy is often thought to be indicated by moderate inflation, which shows steady demand and economic expansion. On the other hand, excessive inflation can destabilize the economy, lower living standards, and erode purchasing power. Deflation, or negative inflation, on the other hand, can be a sign of a faltering economy, impede consumer spending, and deter investment. Policymakers and central banks keep a close eye on inflation data, using it to set monetary policy goals like price stability and inflation targets.

Aside from retail sales, industrial production, and housing starts, other economic indicators provide important information about consumer spending, manufacturing activity, and the state of the real estate market. These indicators provide insights into particular sectors of the economy. Retail sales data monitors the total revenue received by retail establishments and provides information on consumer confidence, spending trends, and general economic mood. The manufacturing, mining, and utility sectors' output is measured as a measure of industrial production, which in turn indicates the state of the industrial sector and overall economic activity. Data on housing starts gives information about how many new residential construction projects were started over a given time period, indicating the health of the housing market, the level of construction activity, and the demand for housing among consumers.

Financial markets may be greatly impacted by the release of economic indicators as investors respond to fresh data regarding the health of the economy. Positive economic news releases, like robust GDP growth or better-than-expected jobless numbers, can boost investor confidence and foster a bullish attitude in the stock market, which raises stock prices. On the other hand, unsatisfactory economic data, like an increase in joblessness or a drop in consumer expenditure, may lead to selling pressure and increased market volatility as investors lower their expectations for the future of the economy.

Central banks and decision-makers in charge of monetary and fiscal policy keep a careful eye on economic indicators. For instance, in order to achieve price stability and encourage economic growth, central banks may use inflation data to set interest rates or modify monetary policy. Similarly, GDP growth data can be used by government officials to evaluate the success of fiscal stimulus plans and modify tax and spending guidelines. Economic indicators give decision-makers important knowledge about the health of the economy, enabling them to create sensible policy responses to deal with problems and promote long-term, sustainable growth.

All things considered, market sentiment, investment choices, and policy decisions are significantly shaped by economic indicators. These indicators assist market participants in navigating the complexities of the global economy and in making well-informed decisions to meet their financial objectives by delivering timely and accurate information about economic conditions. Economic indicators are essential tools for comprehending and interpreting the constantly changing economic landscape, whether they are used to evaluate the state of an economy, direct investment strategies, or inform policy decisions.

Role of Interest Rates and Central Bank Policies

Interest rates and central bank policies wield profound influence over financial Interest rates and central bank policies have a significant impact on financial markets and the economy as a whole, influencing consumer behavior, investment choices, and economic activity as a whole. As the main monetary authorities in the majority of nations, central banks use interest rate policies along with other monetary tools to accomplish a range of policy goals, such as full employment, sustainable economic growth, and price stability.

The determination of interest rates, especially the target for the short-term interbank lending rate, is one of the main ways that central banks exercise their power. Central banks try to affect lending and borrowing behavior by changing interest rates, which has an impact on investment, consumer spending, and overall economic output. Interest rate reductions by central banks make borrowing more affordable, which increases demand for credit and promotes investment and consumption. By increasing aggregate demand, this can support economic growth and mitigate economic downturns. Raising interest rates, on the other hand, makes borrowing more expensive, which can aid in bringing down an overheated economy, containing inflationary pressures, and averting asset bubbles. Central banks aim to accomplish their mandated goals of price stability and sustainable economic growth through the manipulation of interest rates.

To control liquidity in the financial system and affect monetary conditions, central banks use a variety of monetary policy instruments in addition to interest rate setting. For instance, buying and selling government securities on the open market is a form of open market operations. Central banks can alter the amount of liquidity in the banking system through open market operations, which can affect short-term interest rates and the overall monetary environment. Reserve requirements, on the other hand, are another weapon that central banks employ to regulate the money supply and impact lending practices. They specify the quantity of reserves banks must maintain against their deposits.

Moreover, central banks are essential to preserving the integrity of the banking system and preserving financial stability. In order to prevent systemic failures and preserve public confidence in the financial system, central banks may serve as lenders of last resort during periods of financial stress or crisis. They do this by giving banks and other financial institutions liquidity. Central banks can help to stop financial contagion from spreading and stabilize the financial markets during turbulent times by serving as a backstop. To maintain the stability of banks and financial markets and lower the risk of systemic crises, central banks may also enact regulatory and supervisory measures.

The monetary policies implemented by one nation can have a domino effect on other economies and financial markets, meaning that the influence of central bank policies transcends national boundaries. Changes in interest rates by major central banks, like the European Central Bank or the US Federal Reserve, can have an impact on asset prices, exchange rates, and global capital flows. The actions of central banks can also have an impact on investor sentiment and risk appetite, which can cause financial markets to become volatile and have an effect on global economic conditions. In order to support international economic stability, central banks must thus carefully assess the possible knock-on effects of their policies and work in tandem with one another.

The financial markets are particularly affected by interest rates and central bank policies, which have an impact on asset prices, investment choices, and risk management techniques. Interest rate environments can cause investors to reevaluate the relative merits of various asset classes, which can have an impact on the valuation of bonds, stocks, and other financial instruments. Higher interest rates may cause investors to move toward safer assets like bonds, but lower interest rates typically drive up equity prices as they seek higher returns in riskier assets. Furthermore, the market's expectations and investor behavior are greatly influenced by central bank communications and forward guidance. Insights into the future course of monetary policy are frequently provided by central bank officials through speeches, press conferences, and official statements that outline their policy goals and economic outlook. Investors can modify their investment strategies and risk exposures by taking advantage of forward guidance, which serves to stabilize market expectations and lower uncertainty.

In summary, interest rates and central bank policies have a significant impact on how financial markets behave, how the economy functions, and how stable the financial system is. Central banks pursue a number of policy goals, such as price stability, full employment, and sustainable economic growth, by adjusting interest rates and utilizing other monetary tools. Central banks' actions have an impact not only on domestic markets but also on international capital flows, exchange rates, and asset prices. Investors, policymakers, and market participants must comprehend the role of interest rates and central bank policies in order to navigate the complexities of financial markets and make wise decisions in a constantly shifting economic environment.

CHAPTER III

Technical Analysis in Forex Trading

Introduction to Technical Analysis

In the world of trading and investing, technical analysis is essential because it provides traders with a methodical way to interpret market data and make wise decisions. The fundamental idea behind technical analysis is that past price changes, volume, and other market data can provide important clues about how prices may move in the future. Technical analysts seek to gain an advantage in the financial markets by identifying possible trading opportunities through the analysis of patterns, trends, and indicators derived from historical market behavior.

The idea of support and resistance levels is one of the core ideas in technical analysis. Resistance levels indicate price points where selling pressure is expected to be sufficiently strong to impede further price advances, and support levels indicate price levels where buying interest is expected to be sufficiently strong to prevent further price declines. These levels are frequently used by traders to determine possible entry and exit points for their deals as well as to assess the strength of current trends.

Another important component of technical analysis is trend analysis, which tracks and identifies directional price movements over time. In order to profit from future price movements, traders usually try to trade in the direction of the dominant trend. Trends can be categorized as uptrends, downtrends, or sideways trends (ranges). Trends are identified and confirmed using a variety of tools and indicators, including momentum oscillators, trendlines, and moving averages. These tools and indicators give traders important insights into the dynamics of the market.

Technical analysis heavily relies on chart patterns, which provide traders with graphical depictions of market sentiment and possible price movements. These patterns can be anything from straightforward shapes like trendlines and channels to more intricate designs like triangles, flags, pennants, and head and shoulders patterns. Traders can anticipate possible price trend reversals or continuations by identifying these patterns on price charts and modifying their trading strategies accordingly.

Technical analysts use a variety of technical indicators in addition to chart patterns to study market behavior and produce trading signals. These indicators are used to identify trends, momentum, volatility, and other important aspects of market dynamics. They are mathematical computations based on price, volume, or open interest data. Among the many popular technical indicators are moving averages, stochastic oscillators, relative strength index (RSI), and moving average convergence divergence (MACD). These indicators are used by traders to validate trends, spot overbought or oversold situations, and determine when to enter and exit trades.

Technical analysis has its drawbacks and critics, despite offering traders useful tools for examining market data and spotting trading opportunities. Opponents contend that technical analysis lacks a theoretical foundation and that its predictive power is based solely on subjective interpretations of past price data. Furthermore, technical analysis is frequently criticized for failing to take into consideration basic elements that can affect market prices, such as the release of economic data, developments in geopolitics, and central bank policies. Technical analysis is still regarded as a valuable tool by traders and investors in spite of these criticisms because of its ease of use, accessibility, and perceived efficacy in identifying trading opportunities.

To sum up, technical analysis is an effective tool that traders and investors can use to understand market data and make wise choices in the financial markets. Technical analysts look for patterns, trends, and indicators that can offer important clues about future price movements by examining past price movements, volume, and other market data. Despite its drawbacks and detractors, traders and investors continue to favor technical analysis because of its ease of use, accessibility, and perceived efficacy in spotting trading opportunities.

Key Technical Indicators

To make well-informed trading decisions, technical analysis in forex trading significantly depends on important technical indicators. These indicators are crucial tools that traders use to assess price changes, spot patterns, and forecast possible market reversals. For traders hoping to successfully negotiate the intricacies of the forex market, comprehending these indicators and their interpretation is essential.

The moving average is one of the most widely used technical indicators in forex trading. By smoothing out price data over a predetermined time frame, moving averages help traders see the underlying trend more clearly. Moving averages come in various forms, such as exponential moving averages (EMA) and simple moving averages (SMA). Moving averages are frequently used by traders to spot market trends as well as probable levels of support and resistance. Possible trend reversals can also be indicated by crossovers between the long- and short-term moving averages.

The moving average convergence divergence (MACD) is another well-liked technical indicator. The relationship between two moving averages of the price of an asset is measured by the MACD, a trend-following momentum indicator. The signal line and the MACD line make up its two lines. To find possible buying or selling opportunities, traders search for bullish or bearish crossovers between these lines. To further assist traders in determining the strength of a trend, the MACD histogram shows the difference between the signal line and the MACD line visually.

As a momentum oscillator, the relative strength index (RSI) gauges how quickly and how much prices move. The RSI, which has a range of 0 to 100, is commonly employed to determine whether the market is overbought or oversold. A market reversal to the downside may be imminent when the RSI value crosses 70, indicating that the market may be overbought. In contrast, a market reversal to the upside may be imminent if the RSI value drops below 30, which suggests that the market may be oversold. The RSI is used by traders to determine possible entry and exit points as well as to validate the strength of a trend.

Another momentum indicator that's frequently used in forex trading is the stochastic oscillator. The stochastic oscillator gauges overbought and oversold market conditions similarly to the RSI. The %K line and the %D line are its two lines. To find possible buying or selling opportunities, traders search for bullish or bearish crossovers between these lines. Furthermore, possible trend reversals may be indicated by divergences between price movements and the stochastic oscillator.

Three bands make up the Bollinger Band volatility indicator: a middle band, an upper band, and a lower band. The upper and lower bands are standard deviations of the middle band, which is usually a simple moving average. Bollinger Bands give traders a visual depiction of price volatility by expanding and contracting in response to changes in the market. Bollinger Bands are frequently used by traders to spot possible trend reversals when prices approach or surpass the upper or lower bands.

Based on the Fibonacci sequence, Fibonacci retracement levels are a tool for determining possible levels of market support and resistance. On a price chart, traders draw Fibonacci retracement levels to pinpoint potential areas where the price may change course or maintain its current trend. Retracement levels of 23.6%, 38.2%, 50%, 61.8%, and 100% are typical Fibonacci numbers. To confirm possible trading opportunities, traders frequently search for confluence between Fibonacci retracement levels and other technical indicators.

In summary, critical technical indicators are essential to the study of price movements, trend identification, and possible market reversals in forex trading. Among the most popular technical indicators in forex trading are moving averages, MACD, RSI, stochastic oscillator, Bollinger Bands, and Fibonacci retracement levels. Traders can enhance their overall trading performance in the forex market by making well-informed trading decisions and learning how to interpret these indicators.

Chart Patterns and Trends

Understanding technical analysis is essential for traders who want to successfully negotiate the challenging landscape of the forex market. Chart patterns and trends are essential tools in technical analysis that give traders important information about the dynamics of the market and possible price movements. Through comprehension and application of these principles, traders can formulate strong trading plans, recognize profitable prospects, and reduce risks more effectively.

Visual depictions of price changes over time, or chart patterns, can provide hints about the mood of the market and possible future price movements. The head and shoulders pattern is one of the most well-known chart patterns; it usually denotes a trend reversal. Three peaks make up this pattern, with the head—the middle peak—being higher than the other two (the shoulders). A possible downtrend is indicated by a break below the neckline, which is created by joining the lows of the two troughs between the peaks. This pattern is closely watched by traders since it frequently signals important changes in the market.

The double top or double bottom pattern is another frequently seen chart pattern that suggests a possible trend reversal. A double top pattern occurs when the price forms two peaks at roughly the same level in quick succession, then declines below the trough that separates them. On the other hand, a double bottom pattern occurs when the price makes two successive troughs at roughly the same level and then rises above the gapping peak. These patterns frequently act as early warning indicators for traders, indicating a shift in market sentiment.

Another important component of chart analysis is trendlines, which give traders a visual depiction of market trends. Higher highs and lower lows, along with an upward-sloping trendline linking the lows, define an uptrend. On the other hand, a downtrend is characterized by lower highs and lower lows, with a trendline that slopes downward to connect the highs. Trendlines serve as dynamic levels of support and resistance that help traders determine when to enter and exit the market. In order to validate possible trading signals, traders frequently search for confluence between trendlines and other technical indicators.

Traders use technical indicators in addition to chart patterns and trendlines to enhance their analysis and offer extra confirmation signals. For example, moving averages are frequently used to determine the trend's direction and to reduce price swings. As possible entry or exit points, traders frequently search for crossovers between the short- and long-term moving averages. Additionally, oscillators that indicate possible trend reversals, such as the Moving Average Convergence Divergence (MACD) and the Relative Strength Index

(RSI), assist traders in identifying overbought or oversold conditions in the market.

Traders can create successful trading strategies that are suited to their goals and risk tolerance by having a thorough understanding of chart patterns and trends. Traders can predict possible trend reversals and modify their trading positions by recognizing important chart patterns like head and shoulders, double tops or bottoms, and trendlines. Moreover, traders have a thorough framework for examining market trends and arriving at wise trading decisions when they combine technical indicators and chart patterns.

Profitable traders are aware that trends and patterns on charts are useful tools to be used in conjunction with other types of analysis, not as infallible indicators. Traders typically utilize a multifaceted strategy, merging technical, fundamental, and market sentiment analysis to obtain a comprehensive understanding of the market. Traders can improve their capacity to recognize high-probability trading opportunities and efficiently handle risk by combining different analytical techniques.

To sum up, chart patterns and trends are essential to technical analysis and forex trading because they give traders important information about the dynamics of the market and possible price movements. Traders can attain their trading goals and obtain a competitive advantage in the forex market by grasping these ideas and incorporating them into their trading tactics. To make wise trading decisions, traders must, however, proceed with caution and employ chart patterns and trends as a component of a larger analytical framework.

Developing Effective Trading Strategies

It takes a comprehensive understanding of market dynamics, technical analysis methods, risk management principles, and psychological aspects influencing trading decisions to develop successful trading strategies in the forex market. To be successful in this ever-changing market, traders need to take a comprehensive approach, putting different pieces together to create strategies that fit their trading goals and risk tolerance.

Thorough technical analysis is the cornerstone of any successful trading strategy. In order to spot trends, reversals, and possible trading opportunities, technical analysts examine historical price data, chart patterns, and technical indicators. To assess market behavior and make wise decisions, traders employ a variety of instruments and strategies, such as oscillators, trendlines, moving averages, and levels of support and resistance. Traders can gain insights into probable future price movements by analyzing price action and market patterns, which helps them enter and exit trades more precisely.

Robust risk management principles are prioritized by effective trading strategies, in addition to technical analysis. If traders want to continue making money over the long run, they must protect capital and control risk. Traders can reduce potential losses and safeguard their trading capital by using risk management strategies like stop-loss orders, position size limits, and investment diversification. It is possible for traders to reduce the negative effects of unfavorable market movements and preserve a sustainable trading strategy by following strict risk management procedures.

Creating a concise and practical trading plan is an essential part of creating successful trading strategies.

With its detailed entry and exit criteria, risk management guidelines, and profit targets for every trade, a trading plan acts as a road map for traders. Before entering the market, traders should establish their trading goals, time horizon, and risk tolerance. A clear trading plan lowers the possibility of irrational trading behavior and emotional decision-making by assisting traders in maintaining focus, discipline, and consistency. Traders can increase their chances of success in the forex market by executing their strategies with clarity and confidence when they adhere to a structured trading plan.

Effective trading strategies must possess both flexibility and adaptability. Because of the dynamic and ever-changing nature of the forex market, traders must modify their strategies as necessary. Remaining receptive to fresh insights, prepared to reevaluate presumptions, and flexible in their trading strategy are hallmarks of successful traders. Traders can take advantage of new opportunities, handle market swings, and stay ahead of the curve by continuing to be flexible and adaptive.

Creating successful trading strategies requires constant learning and improvement. In order to improve their trading performance, successful traders are dedicated to lifelong learning and self-improvement. They are always looking for new information, abilities, and perspectives. A wide range of educational tools are available to traders to help them improve their trading strategies and gain a deeper understanding of the forex market. These tools include books, webinars, online courses, and mentoring programs. Traders can adjust to shifting market conditions and keep a competitive edge in the market by staying informed and up to date on market developments.

In addition, psychological elements are crucial to the creation of successful trading plans. Irrational behavior in trading can result from emotions like fear, greed, and overconfidence. In times of market turbulence, successful traders overcome psychological obstacles and stay focused by practicing emotional discipline, psychological resilience, and a positive outlook. Traders can learn stress management, impulse control, and maintaining peak performance under pressure by practicing techniques like mindfulness, meditation, and visualization.

To sum up, creating successful trading strategies in the forex market necessitates a thorough strategy that incorporates psychological discipline, technical analysis, risk management, trading planning, flexibility, and ongoing learning. Combining these components allows traders to create strategies that are in line with their goals, increase their chances of success, and confidently and skillfully negotiate the complexities of the forex market. The foundation of effective trading strategies is ultimately comprised of patience, discipline, and a dedication to continuous improvement.

CHAPTER IV

Risk Management in Forex Trading

Importance of Risk Management

Effective risk management is essential to successful forex trading because it safeguards capital, maintains profitability, and ensures long-term viability in the volatile and dynamic forex market. It is impossible to overestimate the significance of risk management since it provides traders with a vital framework for navigating market volatility, averting possible losses, and controlling the inherent risks involved in currency trading.

The intrinsic uncertainty of financial markets is one of the main causes of the critical importance of risk management in forex trading. The forex market is intrinsically dangerous for traders due to its quick price swings, erratic events, and abrupt shifts in market sentiment. Without appropriate risk management procedures in place, traders put themselves at risk of suffering sizable losses that could deplete their trading funds and endanger their capacity to make profitable trades moving forward.

By controlling and limiting their exposure to possible losses, traders can effectively manage risk, protecting their capital and trading funds. Through the application of risk management strategies, such as stop-loss orders, position sizing, and diversification, traders can establish the upper bound of acceptable risk for each trade and guarantee that losses do not surpass their predetermined thresholds. This methodical approach to risk management assists traders in keeping control over their finances and steers clear of emotionally or impulsively driven trading decisions that could result in disastrous losses.

Furthermore, risk management is necessary to guard against unfavorable changes in the market and unforeseen circumstances that could interfere with trading plans and reduce profits. Factors such as market volatility, geopolitical developments, economic data releases, and announcements from central banks can all cause abrupt price fluctuations and have an impact on the value of currencies. Traders can lessen the impact of unfavorable market movements and shield their positions from potential downside risks by utilizing risk management techniques like hedging.

Enhancing traders' psychological health and emotional fortitude in the face of uncertainty and hardship is another important function of risk management. Due to the constant barrage of market fluctuations, swings in profit and loss, and psychological pressures, trading the forex market can be emotionally taxing. Traders who practice effective risk management are better able to control their impulses, keep their emotions in check, and resist giving in to greed, fear, or overconfidence. In order to minimize the emotional toll of trading and promote a successful mindset, traders can navigate market volatility with confidence and composure by managing risk carefully and sticking to their trading plan.

Moreover, maintaining consistency and longevity in forex trading requires effective risk management. The secret to successful trading is consistency, which allows traders to weather the inevitable ups and downs in the market and produce long-term, sustainable returns. Traders can lessen the impact of losing trades, prevent catastrophic drawdowns, and sustain a consistent profit trajectory by putting good risk management practices into place. Maintaining consistency is essential to establishing your reputation as a trader, drawing in clients and investors who respect consistency and dependability in their trading partners.

Furthermore, traders who practice effective risk management are better equipped to take advantage of opportunities and profit from market trends with conviction and confidence. Traders can stay focused on their goals and carry out their plans with accuracy and discipline by taking proactive measures to manage risk and safeguard their capital. This frees traders from the excessive worry of possible losses or unfavorable consequences, enabling them to take measured risks and chase lucrative trading opportunities.

In conclusion, it is impossible to exaggerate the significance of risk management in forex trading. In order to safeguard capital, maintain profitability, control market volatility, uphold emotional control, attain consistency, and take advantage of opportunities in the forex market, effective risk management is crucial. Traders can successfully navigate the challenges of currency trading with confidence, resiliency, and a firm dedication to long-term success by putting good risk management practices into practice. In the end, risk management is the cornerstone of profitable trading strategies, not just a crucial component of successful trading.

Types of Risks in Forex Trading

Success in the field of forex trading largely depends on one's ability to recognize and appropriately manage risks. Forex markets are intrinsically risky environments due to their volatility, liquidity fluctuations, and the impact of numerous economic, political, and social factors. Traders face a variety of risks, each with unique difficulties and ramifications. Through a thorough comprehension of these risks and the application of effective risk management techniques, traders can reduce the possibility of losses, safeguard their capital, and improve their prospects of long-term gains.

The inherent uncertainty surrounding currency price movements in forex trading gives rise to market risk, also known as systematic risk or directional risk. Events in geopolitics, the release of economic data, decisions made by central banks, and shifts in market sentiment are some of the causes of market risk. Currency prices are subject to sudden and sharp fluctuations, which could result in losses for traders who are unable to predict or react appropriately to changes in the market. Traders utilize a variety of strategies, such as position sizing, diversification, and stop-loss orders, to control market risk. Position sizing guarantees that traders risk no more than a predetermined percentage of their capital on each trade, while stop-loss orders help limit losses by automatically closing positions at predetermined price levels. Trading different currency pairs helps spread risk and minimize exposure to any one market or currency. This strategy is known as diversification.

Another important factor to take into account for forex traders is liquidity risk, which is the possibility that there won't be enough market liquidity to allow them to execute trades quickly and at the prices they want. When there is little trading activity, when there are illiquid currency pairs, or when there are market disruptions, liquidity risk can appear. Increased slippage, broader bid-ask spreads, and difficulty entering or exiting positions are all consequences of low liquidity, which can drive up trading costs and expose traders to possible losses. Traders generally stick to trading liquid currency pairs, use limit orders to control execution prices, and concentrate on trading during peak market hours when liquidity is highest in order to manage liquidity risk.

The risk of suffering a financial loss due to a trading counterparty's default or insolvency is commonly referred to as counterparty risk or credit risk. Credit risk in forex trading mostly occurs in over-the-counter (OTC) markets, where trades take place directly between counterparties in the absence of a central clearinghouse. When working with brokers, liquidity providers, or other trading counterparties, traders run the risk of incurring losses if their financial obligations are not met. Traders should monitor credit ratings and financial stability, diversify counterparties to effectively spread risk, and perform thorough due diligence when selecting counterparties in order to mitigate credit risk.

A wide range of risks resulting from internal systems, processes, and human factors in trading operations are included in the category of operational risk. Technological malfunctions, data breaches, fraud, human error, noncompliance with regulations, and other inefficiencies in operations are examples of operational risks. These hazards have the potential to impair trading operations, result in monetary losses, and harm credibility and reputation. Traders should put in place strong internal controls, use backup systems and redundant systems, perform routine audits, and fund employee development in order to reduce operational risk. Traders can minimize disruptions and guarantee the seamless operation of their trading operations by effectively managing operational risks.

The risk of unfavorable regulatory changes or enforcement actions that may have an influence on forex trading operations is known as regulatory risk. Changes in the laws, rules, and policies that control the forex market, such as those pertaining to capital requirements, margin requirements, reporting requirements, and licensing requirements, can result in regulatory risk. Regulations can alter trading circumstances, raise the cost of compliance, and reduce traders' trading options. Traders must adhere to relevant laws and regulations, keep up with regulatory developments, and modify their trading strategies in response to changing regulatory landscapes in order to manage regulatory risk. Furthermore, traders can effectively navigate regulatory challenges by keeping lines of communication open with regulatory authorities and seeking legal advice when needed.

To sum up, there are a variety of risks associated with forex trading, each posing a unique set of difficulties and consequences for traders. Traders can increase their chances of success in the forex market, reduce the possibility of losses, and safeguard their capital by being aware of these risks and putting strong risk management strategies into place. The effective management of risks and the preservation of financial stability and resilience in the face of market volatility require the application of risk management techniques like stop-loss orders, position sizing, diversification, due diligence, and regulatory compliance. In the end, developing effective risk management skills is essential for profitable trading and for attaining long-term sustainability in the forex market.

Position Sizing and Leverage

Leverage and position sizing are two essential elements of risk management techniques used by traders in the forex market to control their exposure to the market and enhance trading performance. The process of figuring out how big a trading position should be based on a variety of variables, including account size, risk tolerance, and market conditions, is known as position sizing. Traders can manage the amount of capital at risk on each trade and make sure that losses are within their risk tolerance levels by appropriately sizing their positions.

Achieving a balance between risk and reward through position sizing allows you to maximize profits while limiting potential losses. Traders usually calculate the size of each position using a percentage of their trading capital, which is referred to as the risk percentage. For instance, if a trader has $10,000 in their account and chooses to risk 1% of that amount on a single trade, they would be risking $100. Traders can prevent overexposure to the market and maintain consistency in their risk management strategy by sticking to a set risk percentage.

Determining the position size based on the distance to the stop-loss level is another important component of position sizing. One of the most important factors in determining the position size is the risk distance, which is the distance from the entry point to the stop-loss level. To calculate the right position size, traders frequently utilize a formula that takes the risk percentage and the risk distance into account. This makes sure that the size of the position is based on the degree of risk involved in each trade; larger position sizes are produced by tighter stop-loss levels and vice versa.

Conversely, leverage is the capacity to manage a bigger position in the market using a smaller amount of capital. By using borrowed money to expand the size of their positions, traders can use leverage to increase their potential returns. Leverage in forex trading is a double-edged sword because, while it can increase profits, it can also increase losses. When using leverage, traders need to be cautious and mindful of the risks.

Leverage and margin trading are closely related. In margin trading, traders must deposit a portion of their entire position size as collateral in order to open and keep a position. Traders' access to leverage varies based on the broker and the jurisdiction; some brokers provide up to 500:1 or greater in leverage. Higher levels of leverage do come with greater risks, though, since trading on margin can turn even tiny price movements into sizable losses.

Achieving a balance between position size and leverage is essential to effective risk management, which allows traders to take advantage of trading opportunities while protecting their capital. While choosing the right amount of leverage and position size for each trade, traders must take into account their trading strategy, risk tolerance, and the state of the market. Increased leverage can result in higher returns, but it also raises the risk of large losses, particularly in erratic market conditions.

Traders should use leverage carefully and refrain from overleveraging their positions in order to reduce the risks involved. Strict risk management procedures should also be followed, such as placing stop-loss orders, diversifying their trading holdings, and refraining from making snap decisions. Traders should also keep a close eye on their positions and modify their risk exposure in response to changes in the market.

To sum up, position sizing and leverage are critical components of forex trading risk management. Traders can control their exposure to the market, safeguard their capital, and improve their chances of success by managing their position sizes and leverage levels well. Traders must, however, use caution and be aware of the risks when utilizing leverage. By putting good risk management techniques into place, traders can position themselves for long-term sustainability and profitability by navigating the complexities of the forex market with confidence and discipline.

Effective Hedging Strategies

In forex trading, effective hedging techniques are essential for controlling risk and safeguarding capital. Taking calculated risks in the market to counteract possible losses from unfavorable price movements in other positions is known as hedging. Hedging tries to reduce downside exposure and protect capital in erratic market conditions, but it does not completely eliminate risk. Traders use a variety of hedging strategies to protect their holdings and successfully manage market volatility.

Using currency pairs with negative correlations is a popular hedging technique in forex trading. When two currency pairs' prices move in opposite directions, it is said to have a negative correlation. Trades can be offset with gains in one position to counteract potential losses in another by simultaneously opening positions in two negatively correlated currency pairs. A trader may open a short position in the USD/CHF pair, which moves inversely to the EUR/USD pair, if they anticipate that their long position in the EUR/USD pair will increase. By doing this, the trader protects themselves from possible losses in the EUR/USD position in the event that the market moves against them.

The ` at the agreed-upon rate. Businesses involved in international trade who want to protect themselves against currency risk related to upcoming transactions can find great value in forward contracts. To mitigate the risk of unfavorable exchange rate movements, a company can enter into a forward contract to sell the foreign currency at a predetermined rate, for instance, if they anticipate receiving payment in that currency in three months.

Another hedging tactic used by traders to guard against currency risk is cross hedging. Using assets or financial instruments that have a strong correlation with the currency pair being traded but are not directly related to it is known as cross hedging. Due to the strong correlation between the Australian dollar (AUD) and the price of gold, a trader holding a long position in the AUD/USD pair may decide to hedge against potential losses by taking a position in gold. The trader can use gains in their gold position to offset potential losses in the AUD/USD pair by taking a position in gold futures or exchange-traded funds (ETFs).

Hedging techniques have their own set of difficulties and factors to take into account, even though they can be useful in reducing risk. One difficulty with hedging is the expense involved, since forward contracts and options contracts usually have fees or premiums. To decide if hedging is a good strategy for their trading goals, traders must assess the costs and potential benefits of the tactic. Hedging can also add layers of complexity and complexity to trading strategies, necessitating constant position monitoring and hedge adjustments as market conditions shift.

Furthermore, since hedging positions may offset gains in other positions, over-hedging can reduce potential profits and limit upside potential. When using hedging strategies, traders need to balance profit generation with risk mitigation. Furthermore, in times of extreme market conditions or high volatility, when correlations between assets may break down, hedging may not always be successful. In these kinds of circumstances, traders need to be ready to modify their hedging plans appropriately and take into account other risk management strategies.

To sum up, proficient hedging tactics are crucial instruments for controlling risk and safeguarding funds in foreign exchange trading. In volatile market conditions, traders can reduce downside risk and protect capital by utilizing strategies like cross-hedging, options contracts, forward contracts, and negatively correlated currency pairs. Traders must, however, carefully consider the advantages and disadvantages of hedging and be ready to modify their plans as market conditions change. Hedging can improve trading performance and help achieve long-term success in the forex market with careful risk management and disciplined execution.

CHAPTER V

Profitable Trading Strategies

Day Trading vs. Swing Trading

In the forex market, day trading and swing trading are two well-liked trading strategies, each with special benefits, drawbacks, and advantages. In day trading, positions are opened and closed within the same trading day with the goal of profiting from intraday volatility and short-term price movements. Conversely, swing trading entails maintaining positions for a few days to a few weeks in an effort to capitalize on market momentum and medium-term price trends. Although there is potential for profit from trading with either approach, different skill sets, approaches, and methods of risk management are needed.

Traders who like the thrill of intraday market movements and who do well in fast-paced environments will find day trading appealing. In order to spot short-term trading opportunities, day traders keep a close eye on price charts, technical indicators, and market news. They frequently execute several trades during the day. Making money from quick changes in price and taking advantage of small price variations are the main objectives of day trading. Tight stop-loss orders are usually used by day traders to restrict possible losses, and they follow stringent risk management guidelines to safeguard their capital. Day trading necessitates quick decision-making abilities, discipline, and effective emotion management due to the high frequency of trades.

The ability to make large returns on investment and fast profits is one of day trading's main benefits. Day traders can make sizable profits from several trades made throughout the day because their goal is to profit from slight price movements. Additionally, day trading shields traders from overnight exposure to market risks like unforeseen news releases or geopolitical shifts that could affect positions held overnight. Furthermore, day trading gives traders flexibility and enables them to modify their strategies in response to shifting market conditions in order to take advantage of intraday trends and opportunities.

But there are risks and difficulties unique to day trading. Since day traders have to keep an eye on price movements and execute trades fast and precisely, one of the biggest challenges is the requirement for intense concentration and focus. If day trading is not properly managed, its fast-paced nature can be emotionally and mentally taxing, resulting in stress and exhaustion. Additionally, day traders are vulnerable to abrupt price reversals and market volatility, which can cause large losses if trades are not properly timed or managed.

Furthermore, day traders may incur additional costs as a result of needing access to fast execution platforms, dependable internet connections, and real-time market data.

Conversely, swing traders are more appealing to those who want a more laid-back trading style and are prepared to hold positions longer in order to take advantage of medium-term price trends. In order to spot possible trend reversals or continuation patterns, swing traders examine price charts, technical indicators, and market fundamentals. Their goal is to enter positions at the best possible times and ride the trend until it loses steam. Swing traders, in contrast to day traders, don't care about intraday price swings and are prepared to put up with brief market volatility in order to take advantage of longer-term market trends. Patience, discipline, and a deep comprehension of market dynamics are necessary for swing trading.

The potential for higher profits than day trading is one of swing trading's main benefits. Swing traders can profit from significant price movements and increase their return on investment because their goal is to capture medium-term price trends. Additionally, swing trading enables traders to benefit from trend-following techniques and market momentum, which can lead to profitable trades over an extended period of time. Furthermore, swing trading is more flexible and takes less time than day trading, which makes it appropriate for traders who have other obligations or hectic schedules.

But swing trading has its own set of difficulties and dangers. The primary difficulty for swing traders is that they have to wait for price trends to develop and resist the urge to close positions too soon. Swing traders must be able to endure brief market ups and downs without losing heart or straying from their strategy. Additionally, swing traders are vulnerable to risks associated with the overnight market, like gap openings and unfavorable news releases, which can lead to large losses if positions are not handled correctly. Furthermore, because swing trading involves longer holding periods, traders must set wider stop-loss orders and risk management parameters, which may have an impact on risk-reward ratios and profit potential.

In conclusion, there are two different ways to trade the forex market: swing trading and day trading. Both present different chances and difficulties for traders. Swing trading seeks to profit from medium-term price trends and market momentum, whereas day trading concentrates on capturing short-term price movements and intraday volatility. Before selecting a trading style, traders should carefully consider their trading goals, risk tolerance, and time commitment. Both approaches require different skill sets, strategies, and risk management techniques. Traders can increase their chances of success in the forex market by learning the traits of swing and day trading and putting these traits into practice.

Trend Following Strategies

In forex trading, trend-following strategies are a common method that concentrate on spotting and capitalizing on market trends. These strategies are predicated on the idea that markets frequently follow enduring trends, and that traders can profit from these trends by anticipating future price movements. Technical analysis tools and indicators are used by trend following strategies to determine trend direction, entry and exit points, and risk management parameters. Trend-following strategies are especially useful for identifying medium- to long-term trends in the forex market, even though they can be used on a variety of timeframes.

The idea of trend identification is one of the foundational ideas of trend following tactics. Moving averages, trendlines, and price channels are examples of technical analysis tools that traders use to determine the direction and strength of a market trend. For example, moving averages are frequently used to smooth price data and offer a visual depiction of trend direction. Combining short- and long-term moving averages can help traders confirm trend direction and reduce noise from market fluctuations. In order to visualize the trajectory of price movements, traders can draw lines connecting successive highs or lows using trendlines and price channels, which are also useful tools for determining trend direction.

Trend following strategies concentrate on entering positions in the trend's direction after a trend has been identified. To enter trades at the best times, traders can employ a variety of entry strategies, including breakouts, pullbacks, and trend continuation patterns. Using breakout strategies, trades are placed when the price breaks out above or below important levels of support or resistance, suggesting that the trend may continue. Conversely, pullback strategies entail making trades during brief retracements or pullbacks within the trend with the goal of profiting from advantageous entry points with lower risk. Additionally, trustworthy entry signals that denote a resumption of the underlying trend can be obtained from trend continuation patterns like triangles, pennants, and flags.

A key component of trend-following strategies is risk management, which aids traders in safeguarding their investment and controlling possible losses. Stop-loss orders are usually used by traders to reduce the amount of risk they take on and to exit positions if the market moves against them. To specify the maximum allowable loss for each trade, stop-loss orders are placed above or below important resistance or support levels, depending on whether the trader is buying or selling. Furthermore, traders can modify the size of their positions according to the degree of risk and the separation from the stop-loss level by employing position sizing strategies. In times of market volatility, traders can reduce losses and protect capital by putting effective risk management strategies into place.

Trade management, which entails tracking and modifying trades as the market changes, is another crucial element of trend-following tactics. Trailing stop-loss orders are a tool that traders can use to secure profits and preserve gains when the market turns in their favor. Trailing stops enable traders to profit from possible gains while guarding against unfavorable price reversals. They do this by automatically adjusting to follow the movement of the market. In addition, traders can scale out of positions gradually as the trend develops, taking partial profits along the way, by using multiple profit targets. Traders can optimize their profits and adjust to shifting market conditions by actively managing their trades.

Trend following strategies have drawbacks and difficulties that traders should be aware of despite their possible advantages. A problem that can arise is the existence of whipsaws, or false signals, in which brief price fluctuations in the market cause signals to enter or exit the market too soon. Traders can lessen this risk by validating trend signals and lowering the possibility of false signals by adding more filters or confirmation indicators. Additionally, in range-bound situations or times of market consolidation, when trends are less prominent, trend-following strategies may perform poorly or even lose money. In these times, traders might have to modify their plans or use different tactics in order to react to shifting market conditions.

In summary, trend-following strategies are a well-liked and successful method in forex trading that gives traders the chance to profit from medium- to long-term market trends. In order to determine trend direction, entry and exit points, and risk management parameters, these strategies rely on technical analysis tools. In the forex market, traders can potentially make consistent profits by adhering to established trends and putting effective risk management strategies into place. It is imperative to acknowledge the constraints and difficulties associated with trend-following tactics and modify tactics in response to evolving market circumstances. Trend following strategies can be useful instruments for traders trying to make sense of the intricacies of the forex market, provided they are applied with appropriate analysis, discipline, and risk management.

Range Trading Strategies

Forex traders frequently employ range trading strategies to profit from times of market consolidation or sideways price movements. Range trading strategies concentrate on locating and trading within particular price ranges or boundaries, as opposed to trend following strategies, which seek to capture directional price movements. These trading methods are predicated on the idea that prices frequently fluctuate between levels of support and resistance. This provides traders with trading opportunities, provided they can recognize these ranges and place trades appropriately.

Finding levels of support and resistance is one of the main tenets of range trading strategies. Support levels are places where the selling pressure is greater than the buying interest, halting further price declines. Conversely, resistance levels show places where there is more selling pressure than buying interest, which stops prices from going higher. To find these crucial levels, traders employ a variety of technical analysis instruments and indicators, including pivot points, Bollinger Bands, and horizontal support and resistance lines. Through the examination of past price data, traders can determine the limits of the trading range and predict possible trading opportunities by identifying key price levels that have historically seen price reversals.

Range trading strategies concentrate on buying close to support levels and selling close to resistance levels once the trading range has been determined. Traders can take advantage of price movements within the range by using various entry and exit strategies. In anticipation of a price bounce or reversal higher, traders might, for instance, enter long positions when prices approach support levels and exit them when prices reach resistance levels. On the other hand, as prices get closer to resistance levels, traders may initiate short positions in anticipation of a decline or reversal, and they may exit these positions when prices get closer to support levels. Traders who stay inside the defined range try to capitalize on price fluctuations without having to guess which way the next big trend will go.

Range trading strategies require traders to manage risk because they need to be ready for breakouts or false signals that could happen inside the trading range. Stop-loss orders are usually used by traders to reduce the amount of risk they take on and to exit positions if the market moves against them. In order to specify the highest allowable loss for each trade, stop-loss orders are placed outside the trading range, past the levels of support and resistance. Furthermore, traders can modify the size of their positions according to the degree of risk and the separation from the stop-loss level by employing position sizing strategies. In times of market volatility, traders can reduce losses and protect capital by putting effective risk management strategies into place.

Trade management, which entails keeping an eye on and modifying trades as the market changes, is another crucial factor to take into account when developing a range trading strategy. To lock in profits and safeguard gains as prices move within the trading range, traders can employ trailing stop-loss orders or profit targets. Traders can take profits when prices hit profit targets, which are predefined levels based on range boundaries or other technical indicators. Trailing stop-loss orders enable traders to profit from possible gains while guarding against unfavorable price reversals. They automatically adapt to the movement of the market. Additionally, as prices move within the range, traders can use multiple profit targets to scale out of positions gradually, taking partial profits along the way. Traders can optimize their profits and adjust to shifting market conditions by actively managing their trades.

Range trading strategies have drawbacks and difficulties that traders should be aware of despite their possible advantages. A problem that can arise is the occurrence of false breakouts or whipsaws, in which prices move outside of the trading range for a short while before turning back. Traders may suffer losses as a result of these false signals, which can also cause early entry or exit signals. Traders can lessen the chance of false breakouts and validate trading signals by using additional filters or confirmation indicators. Furthermore, range trading strategies can lose money or perform poorly when there is a lot of market volatility or when the market moves from a ranging to a trending phase. In these times, traders might have to modify their plans or use different tactics in order to react to shifting market conditions.

Finally, range trading strategies are an effective method for forex traders looking to profit from sideways price movements or periods of market consolidation. These strategies, which are predicated on the idea that prices frequently oscillate between support and resistance levels, concentrate on locating and trading within particular price ranges or boundaries. In range-bound markets, traders can potentially make consistent profits by actively managing trades, putting risk management strategies into place, and accurately identifying support and resistance levels. It is imperative to acknowledge the constraints and difficulties associated with range trading tactics and modify tactics in response to evolving market circumstances. Range trading strategies can be useful tools for traders attempting to navigate the complexities of the forex market if they are properly analyzed, disciplined, and risk managed.

Breakout Trading Strategies

Forex traders frequently employ breakout trading strategies to profit from large price movements that happen when an asset's price breaks out of a predetermined trading range or consolidation pattern. Breakout trading strategies concentrate on seizing the possible momentum and volatility that come along with breakout events, as opposed to range trading strategies, which seek to profit from price oscillations within a range. These trading strategies are predicated on the idea that price breakouts frequently herald the start of fresh trends or the extension of current ones, giving traders the chance to enter positions in the breakout's direction and possibly profit from robust price momentum.

Finding breakout patterns and chart formations is a fundamental component of breakout trading strategies. To find possible breakout setups, traders employ a variety of technical analysis tools and indicators, including trendlines, support and resistance levels, triangle, rectangle, and wedge chart patterns, and momentum oscillators, such as the Moving Average Convergence Divergence (MACD) and the Relative Strength Index (RSI). Usually, breakout patterns emerge following a phase of sideways or consolidation, during which prices are trapped in a small trading range. When prices break out of these consolidation patterns, traders look to enter trades as this could indicate the start of a new trend or the continuation of an already established one.

Breakout trading strategies concentrate on placing trades in the breakout's direction after a breakout pattern has been identified. To enter trades at advantageous prices, traders can employ a variety of entry strategies, including breakout pullbacks, break retests, and breakouts on high volume. In order to increase trading opportunities and lower the possibility of false breakouts, breakout pullbacks entail waiting for prices to retreat to the breakout level before making a trade. When prices retest the breakout level following the initial breakout, this is known as a break retest. It gives traders a chance to enter trades at the retest level once the breakout has been confirmed. High volume breakouts are regarded as more trustworthy because they show significant market participation and conviction in the breakout move.

Because traders need to be ready for whipsaws and false breakouts, risk management is an essential component of breakout trading strategies. When prices move past the breakout level for a brief period of time before turning back, it is known as a false breakout. This traps traders who made trades too soon. Traders usually use stop-loss orders to exit trades if the market moves against them in order to reduce this risk. In order to limit losses and protect capital in the event of a false breakout, traders can place stop-loss orders above the breakout level for short trades and below it for long trades. Furthermore, traders can modify the size of their positions according to the degree of risk and the separation from the stop-loss level by employing position sizing strategies.

Another crucial factor in breakout trading strategies is trade management, since traders need to keep an eye on their positions and adjust them as the market moves. As prices move closer to the breakout, traders can use trailing stop-loss orders or profit targets to lock in profits and preserve gains. Traders are able to take profits when prices hit these predefined levels because profit targets are set based on technical analysis, Fibonacci extensions, or previous swing highs or lows. Trailing stop-loss orders enable traders to profit from possible gains while guarding against unfavorable price reversals. They automatically adapt to the movement of the market.

Breakout trading strategies have drawbacks and difficulties that traders should be aware of despite their possible advantages. False breakouts or whipsaws are a problem that can arise often, particularly in volatile or fluctuating market conditions. Traders may suffer losses as a result of these false signals, which can also cause early entry or exit signals. Traders can lessen the chance of false breakouts by validating breakout signals with additional filters or confirmation indicators. Furthermore, breakout trading strategies might lose money or perform poorly when the market moves from a trending to a ranging phase or when there is little volatility. In these times, traders might have to modify their plans or use different tactics in order to react to shifting market conditions.

Finally, for forex traders looking to profit from large price movements that happen when prices break out of consolidation patterns, breakout trading strategies are a useful tactic. Based on the idea that breakout events frequently indicate the emergence of new trends or the continuation of existing ones, these strategies concentrate on spotting and entering trades in the direction of breakouts. In breakout markets, traders can potentially make consistent profits by actively managing trades, implementing risk management strategies, and effectively identifying breakout patterns. It is imperative to acknowledge the constraints and difficulties associated with breakout trading tactics and modify tactics in response to evolving market circumstances. Breakout trading strategies can be useful tools for traders attempting to navigate the complexities of the forex market if they are applied properly, with discipline, analysis, and risk management.

CHAPTER VI

Trading Psychology

Understanding Emotions in Trading

For forex traders hoping to achieve sustained success in the financial markets, it is essential to comprehend emotions in trading. An important factor in determining traders' decisions, behavior, and ultimately trading results is emotion. Emotions like fear, greed, hope, and regret can cause traders to make rash or illogical trading decisions that could hurt their performance and result in losses. To maintain discipline, effectively manage risk, and make well-informed decisions, traders must therefore master the psychological aspects of trading and develop emotional intelligence.

One of the most frequent feelings that traders go through is fear, which can make decisions completely incapacitated. Even when a trader's trading strategy clearly indicates a profitable opportunity, traders may hesitate or avoid making trades altogether out of fear of losing money. Traders may be unable to adhere to their predetermined risk management guidelines or to their trading plan as a result of this fear of failing or loss aversion. To get over their fear of losing money, traders need to learn to accept that losses are a necessary part of the process and concentrate on managing their risk and trade execution rather than worrying about uncontrollable events.

The strong emotion of greed is another one that can impair traders' judgment and cause them to make illogical decisions. Traders may stray from their trading plan and incur excessive risk due to the temptation to chase winning trades or the need for rapid profits. Several behaviors are indicative of greed, including overtrading, hanging onto losing positions in the hopes of a reversal, and taking on larger-than-sensible position sizes. In order to combat greed, traders need to develop self-control, patience, and a logical trading strategy. A balanced and long-term trading strategy can be maintained by traders by establishing reasonable profit targets, abiding by risk management guidelines, and refraining from snap judgments motivated by greed.

Clinging to losing positions in the hopes of a miraculous recovery or reversal is a psychological trap known as hope. Due to their overly optimistic outlook, traders may disregard cautionary signals, justify bad choices, and put off taking the required steps to reduce losses and protect capital. While it's important to stay confident in your trading approach, trading performance can suffer from blind optimism. Traders need to be able to distinguish between hope and a realistic assessment of the state of the market, analyze their trades objectively, and act decisively when necessary to limit losses and safeguard their capital.

After placing a losing trade or passing up a lucrative opportunity, traders frequently feel regret. Traders may have regrets about past choices, which can cause them to feel irritated, disappointed, or insecure. A vicious cycle of indecision and additional losses can arise from traders dwelling on past transgressions or lost opportunities, which impairs judgment and undermines confidence. In order to overcome trading regret, traders need to focus on continuous improvement, have a growth mindset, and see losses and setbacks as teaching moments. Traders can get past regret and proceed with clarity and confidence by keeping a positive outlook, learning from their mistakes, and focusing on the here and now.

Self-awareness, emotional intelligence, and mental toughness are necessary for managing emotions in trading. Traders need to learn how to identify and manage emotional triggers, remain disciplined under duress, and maintain focus on their long-term objectives. Traders can maintain composure and focus during times of market turbulence or uncertainty by using strategies like mindfulness, visualization, and relaxation exercises. Traders can also manage stress and preserve emotional well-being by doing self-care activities outside of trading, pursuing peer or mentor support, and keeping a healthy work-life balance.

To sum up, in order for forex traders to successfully negotiate the intricacies of the financial markets, they must have a solid understanding of emotions in trading. Fear, greed, hope, regret, and other strong emotions can affect traders' decisions and trading results. Traders can remain disciplined, effectively manage risk, and make well-informed decisions by refining their psychological aspects of trading, developing emotional intelligence, and putting effective coping mechanisms into practice. The bottom line is that traders can improve their performance and find long-term success in the forex market by developing resilience, self-awareness, and a balanced mindset.

Overcoming Psychological Biases

Overcoming psychological prejudices is a vital component of profitable forex trading. Psychological biases are innate inclinations or mental short cuts that affect traders' decision-making and may result in less-than-ideal results. These psychological biases can take many different forms, including loss aversion, confirmation bias, anchoring, and overconfidence. It is crucial for traders to identify and overcome these biases in order to make logical, well-researched decisions and consistently turn a profit from their trading endeavors.

Overconfidence is one of the most prevalent psychological biases among traders, which causes them to overestimate their skills and underestimate risks. Overconfident traders run the risk of losing money by trading impulsively, taking on too much risk, or failing to follow appropriate risk management procedures. Traders who want to overcome overconfidence need to develop humility and take an honest look at their abilities and limitations. This entails owning up to past errors, asking mentors or peers for advice, and always aiming to increase one's trading expertise. Traders can lessen the negative effects of overconfidence and make better trading decisions by retaining a healthy dose of skepticism and remaining grounded in reality.

Another common psychological bias that can impair traders' objectivity and result in biased decision-making is confirmation bias. Confirmation bias happens when traders ignore or reject evidence that contradicts their preconceived notions or biases in favor of information that supports them. Due to this bias, traders may be unable to fully analyze the situation or take into account opposing viewpoints, which could result in poor trading decisions. Traders need to actively seek out different perspectives and information sources while maintaining an open mind in order to overcome confirmation bias. Traders can make more objective and informed decisions by testing their hypotheses, challenging their assumptions, and taking a variety of factors into account.

A cognitive bias known as "anchoring" happens when traders become fixated on particular prices or reference points and then use those points to gauge how the market will move in the future. In order to avoid making unbiased interpretations of market data and trading decisions, traders may base their expectations on historical price levels, recent highs or lows, or analyst projections. Traders need to have a flexible mindset and refrain from depending too much on fixed reference points in order to combat anchoring bias. Rather, in order to make unbiased trading decisions, traders ought to concentrate on examining the state of the market, trends, and price action. Traders can lessen the impact of anchoring bias and make more accurate assessments of market dynamics by remaining flexible and receptive to new information.

A psychological bias known as loss aversion makes traders more sensitive to the agony of losses than the joy of gains, which discourages them from taking on unnecessary risk or from exiting positions too soon. Even when their trading strategy indicates a clear opportunity, loss-averse traders may avoid entering trades altogether or hang onto losing positions in the hopes of a turnaround. Traders need to embrace losses as a necessary component of the trading process and take a disciplined approach to risk management in order to overcome loss aversion. Traders can lessen the negative effects of loss aversion and enhance their overall trading performance by establishing predetermined risk parameters, following stop-loss levels, and concentrating on long-term performance rather than individual trades.

A further psychological bias that may impact traders is the disposition effect, or the propensity to hang onto profitable trades for an extended period of time and cut losses prematurely. This bias results from a desire to keep control over one's investments and to avoid regret. Disposition effect, however, can result in lost opportunities and less than ideal trading results. Instead of allowing their emotions to control their decisions, traders need to overcome the disposition effect by concentrating on adhering to their trading plan and specified exit criteria. Traders can improve their trading performance over time and prevent the disposition effect by adhering to a disciplined and consistent trading approach.

To sum up, traders must overcome psychological biases in order to succeed in the forex market. Traders can make more logical, disciplined decisions and perform better overall by identifying and addressing biases like confirmation bias, overconfidence, anchoring, loss aversion, and the disposition effect. By means of self-awareness, emotional intelligence, and a dedication to ongoing education and advancement, traders can surmount psychological prejudices and cultivate the mental fortitude required to prosper in the ever-changing and demanding realm of foreign exchange trading.

Developing Discipline and Patience

For forex traders hoping to successfully navigate the complexities of the financial markets and attain long-term success, cultivating discipline and patience is essential. The ability to follow set rules and guidelines, stick to a structured trading plan, and trade consistently is referred to as discipline. Conversely, patience entails waiting for trading opportunities with a high probability of success, being restrained when faced with uncertainty, and refraining from making snap decisions. In the dynamic and frequently unpredictable world of forex trading, discipline and patience are two critical traits that can aid traders in overcoming psychological obstacles, effectively managing risk, and maintaining a resilient mindset.

A fundamental component of successful trading is discipline, which gives traders the structure and framework they need to execute trades precisely and make well-informed decisions. A well-defined trading plan outlining precise entry and exit criteria, guidelines for risk management, and overall trading goals is adhered to by a disciplined trader. Traders can minimize the impact of psychological biases, steer clear of emotional decisions, and stay focused on their long-term objectives by consistently following their plan. Maintaining a high degree of emotional and self-control is another aspect of discipline, particularly in times of uncertainty or market volatility. Disciplined traders are able to make logical decisions based on reasoning and analysis rather than giving in to fear or greed when faced with pressure by maintaining their composure.

It takes commitment, diligence, and a willingness to follow set procedures and guidelines to develop trading discipline. In order to achieve their trading objectives, traders need to develop wholesome routines and habits. Some examples of these include reviewing previous trades to pinpoint areas for improvement, regularly analyzing the market, and keeping a trading journal to track performance. As traders must show that they can stick to their trading plan over time, regardless of short-term fluctuations or setbacks, consistency is essential to developing discipline. Trades can increase their self-confidence, sharpen their decision-making abilities, and eventually succeed more in the forex market by maintaining a disciplined approach to trading.

Patience is another crucial quality that can have a big impact on a trader's success in the forex market, along with discipline. The ability to wait for good trading opportunities to arise, as opposed to making snap decisions or going after fast gains, is a sign of patience. Patient traders are prepared to wait for the ideal circumstances to arise before making a trade because they are aware that successful trading takes patience, hard work, and meticulous planning. The ability to manage trades once they are open requires patience as well, since traders must fight the impulse to enter the market too soon or to exit positions in response to momentary swings. Traders can improve their long-term odds of success and steer clear of emotional decision-making by being patient and letting deals play out as planned.

In order to trade with patience, one must change their perspective from one of immediate gratification to one of long-term planning and delayed rewards. It is imperative for traders to acknowledge that trading is an inescapable aspect of the process and that not every trading opportunity will yield instant profits. Patient traders see losses as important teaching moments that present chances for development and improvement rather than giving up easily. Remaining realistic about market expectations and resisting the need to overtrade or take unwarranted risks in the hopes of making quick gains are other aspects of patience. Through the practice of patient trading, traders can develop resilience, boost their self-assurance, and attain long-term profitability in the foreign exchange market.

Being well-prepared and educated is one of the best ways to cultivate discipline and patience in trading. It takes time for traders to become knowledgeable about the fundamentals of forex trading, comprehend the workings of the market, and hone their trading methods. Through education, traders can acquire the knowledge and abilities necessary to confidently negotiate the complexities of the forex market and make well-informed decisions based on solid analysis. Traders should also exercise patience by beginning with modest position sizes, emphasizing quality above quantity, and progressively raising their risk tolerance as they acquire expertise and self-assurance. Traders can develop patience and discipline over time and position themselves for long-term success in the forex market by approaching trading methodically and gradually.

Moreover, continuous self-awareness and introspection are necessary to sustain patience and discipline. In order to spot areas where they might be more likely to lose control or become impatient, traders need to routinely evaluate their emotions, biases, and behaviors. By identifying these patterns, traders can put countermeasures in place. Some of these include taking breaks from trading when feeling anxious or overwhelmed, managing emotions with mindfulness and relaxation exercises, and asking for help from trading communities or mentors. Trading professionals should also adopt a growth mindset and see failures as chances for growth and development rather than as mistakes. Traders can develop their patience and discipline and eventually become more successful traders by accepting challenges and staying strong in the face of difficulty.

To sum up, in order for forex traders to successfully navigate the complexities of the financial markets and attain long-term success, they must cultivate discipline and patience. Following a set trading plan, being consistent in one's approach, and practicing self-control and emotional regulation are all examples of discipline. Waiting for excellent trading opportunities, handling trades coolly and sensibly, and taking a long-term view of trading success are all components of patience. Through education, planning, self-awareness, and resilience, traders can develop discipline and patience, which will help them make better decisions and eventually reach their objectives in the forex market.

Maintaining Emotional Stability During Trades

Maintaining emotional composure while trading is essential for forex market success. Effective risk management, sound decision-making, and long-term profitability all depend on one's capacity to maintain composure in the face of trading's volatility and uncertainty. This section will look at the psychological difficulties that traders encounter, the value of emotional stability in trading, and some doable tactics for building and preserving emotional resilience in the fast-paced world of forex trading.

The ability to regulate one's emotions, including fear, greed, and anxiety, and to sustain a stable psychological state during trading is referred to as emotional stability in trading. Human nature is emotional, and emotions have a big influence on decisions, especially when there's a lot of pressure involved, like trading. While greed can lead to chasing profits and taking unwarranted risks, fear of losses may cause impulsive selling. Furthermore, tension and worry can impair judgment and interfere with reasoned thought. Therefore, in order for traders to successfully navigate the challenges of the forex market, emotional stability must be developed.

Fear of losing money is one of the main psychological issues that traders face. Fear of losing money can set off a chain reaction of emotions that can lead to poor trading results and impaired decision-making, such as panic, anxiety, and hesitation. In order to overcome this obstacle, traders must accept that losses in trading are inevitable and implement a disciplined approach to risk management. Traders can lessen the fear and impact of losses by employing appropriate risk management strategies, such as sizing positions appropriately, diversifying holdings, and setting stop-loss orders.

Traders frequently face the psychological obstacle of the desire to pursue profits or engage in revenge trading following losses. This conduct is motivated by the need to quickly recover losses or profit from winning streaks, which frequently leads to rash and unreasonable choices. Traders need to develop patience and discipline in their trading approach in order to stay out of this trap. Traders should concentrate on sticking to their trading plan, staying consistent with their strategies, and accepting losses as a necessary part of the trading process rather than chasing profits or seeking retribution. Traders can steer clear of emotional traps and make more logical trading decisions by maintaining discipline and patience.

In addition, traders frequently find it difficult to control their emotions when there is market turbulence or unexpected news breaks. Increased emotions brought on by market volatility can result in rash decisions and unpredictable trading behavior. Traders should concentrate on staying informed, keeping perspective, and avoiding rash decisions in order to maintain emotional stability during volatile market conditions. Furthermore, traders can handle erratic markets with confidence and discipline if they have a clear trading plan with predetermined entry and exit

Pre-trade routines, relaxation exercises, and seeking out social support are useful tactics for preserving emotional stability during trades. Pre-trade rituals can aid traders in mentally and emotionally getting ready for the upcoming trading day. Some of these routines include performing in-depth market analysis, establishing reasonable trading goals, and visualizing profitable trades. Additionally, reducing stress and promoting emotional balance during trades can be achieved by engaging in relaxation techniques like yoga, meditation, or deep breathing exercises. Lastly, when things get tough, asking for social support from other traders, friends, or family can offer consolation, perspective, and encouragement.

In conclusion, emotional composure is a critical component of successful trading in the foreign exchange market. Through the regulation of emotions, handling of psychological obstacles, and application of pragmatic tactics, traders can improve their ability to make decisions, efficiently handle risk, and attain sustained financial gains. It takes time, effort, and practice to become emotionally resilient, but it is a worthwhile endeavor for traders who want to succeed in the fast-paced, unpredictable world of forex trading. Traders can develop their confidence, get past challenges, and reach their full potential by putting emotional stability first.

CHAPTER VII

Advanced Trading Techniques

Introduction to Algorithmic Trading

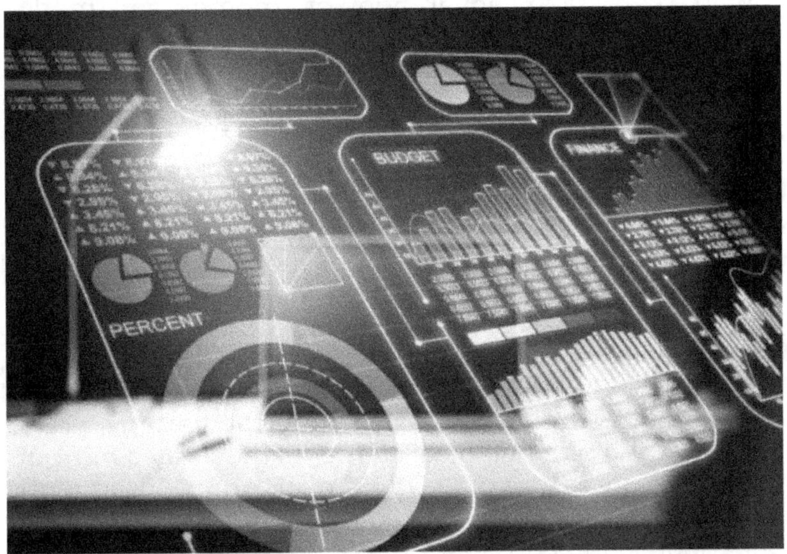

The Introduction of algorithmic trading represents a major development in the field of financial markets, including the foreign exchange market. Algorithmic trading, also referred to as automated trading or black-box trading, is the process of executing trades using computer algorithms in accordance with pre-established standards and directives. These algorithms are made to evaluate market data, spot trading opportunities, and quickly and accurately execute trades—often without the need for human involvement. With its many benefits, including enhanced risk management, lower transaction costs, and greater efficiency, algorithmic trading has completely changed the way that trades are made.

The capacity of algorithmic trading to execute trades at speeds significantly faster than those of humans is one of its main advantages. Because algorithms can complete trades in milliseconds or microseconds, algorithmic traders can take advantage of momentary market opportunities that human traders might miss. In high-frequency trading (HFT), where traders seek to profit from minute price fluctuations in the market, this speed advantage is especially important. Rapid-fire trading strategies can yield substantial profits for HFT firms by utilizing algorithms to execute trades at breakneck speed.

Additionally, traders can execute trades consistently and precisely with algorithmic trading, independent of human emotions and biases. In contrast to human traders who could be influenced by greed, fear, or other feelings, algorithms follow predetermined guidelines and standards to the letter. This methodical strategy aids in removing the psychological elements that may contribute to rash or unreasonable trading decisions. Consequently, over time, algorithmic trading may produce more dependable and consistent trading results.

Algorithmic trading also has the benefit of automating intricate trading procedures and strategies. Traders can automate the entire trading process, from market analysis to trade execution, by encoding trading rules and strategies into algorithms. In addition to saving time and effort, this automation enables traders to execute trades simultaneously across a number of markets and instruments. Algorithms also have the ability to continuously monitor market conditions and modify trading parameters in response, giving traders a flexible and dynamic trading strategy.

When compared to manual trading, algorithmic trading also provides better risk management capabilities. Risk management parameters that algorithms can use in their trading strategies include position sizing, risk limits, and stop-loss orders. This guarantees that trades are carried out within reasonable risk parameters and lessens the possibility of significant losses. Algorithms can also track portfolio diversification and exposure, which aids traders in keeping a well-managed and balanced portfolio.

Aside from these advantages, leveling the playing field for traders of all sizes is another way that algorithmic trading has democratized access to the financial markets. Large institutional investors with the means to create complex trading algorithms used to be the main users of algorithmic trading. But now that online trading platforms have proliferated and technology has advanced, algorithmic trading is also available to retail traders. Retail traders can now automate their trading strategies and increase their competitiveness in the market by using a variety of algorithmic trading tools and platforms.

Algorithmic trading has many benefits, but there are also some risks and difficulties that traders need to be aware of. A primary obstacle is the intricacy involved in creating and executing efficient trading algorithms. A thorough grasp of technical analysis, programming languages, and market dynamics are necessary for creating reliable algorithms. In order to guarantee algorithms' efficacy and dependability under various market circumstances, they also need to undergo extensive testing and optimization.

Furthermore, algorithmic trading may be vulnerable to system malfunctions and technical issues, which, if improperly handled, could cause large losses. For instance, a broken algorithm could result in unanticipated losses by executing trades incorrectly or failing to react to shifting market conditions. Traders need to put strong risk management procedures in place, maintain their systems on a regular basis, and keep a careful eye on algorithm performance in order to reduce this risk.

Concerns regarding market fairness and integrity have also been brought up by algorithmic trading, especially in the context of high-frequency trading. High-frequency traders are criticized for potentially unfairly gaining an advantage over other market participants and for adding to market instability due to their superior speed and technological capabilities. In response to these worries, regulators have put policies in place to improve market transparency, keep an eye on algorithmic trading activity, and stop market manipulation.

In summary, algorithmic trading is a huge development in the forex market that has many advantages, including improved speed, accuracy, and efficiency. Trades can be executed quickly, consistently, and precisely by using computer algorithms to automate trading procedures. This also helps traders manage risk better. Algorithmic trading does, however, come with some risks and difficulties, such as the difficulty of creating efficient algorithms, technological hiccups, and issues with market integrity. In order to fully capitalize on algorithmic trading, traders need to be aware of its advantages and disadvantages, put strong risk management procedures in place, and keep a close eye on algorithm performance.

High-Frequency Trading Strategies

High-frequency trading (HFT) strategies, which use cutting-edge technology and algorithms to execute trades at breakneck speeds, have completely changed the nature of financial markets, including the forex market. With these strategies, a multitude of trades can be executed in a matter of milliseconds by analyzing market data and identifying short-term trading opportunities using complex computer algorithms. High frequency trading (HFT) strategies are distinguished by their rapidity, high turnover rates, and brief holding times—often measured in milliseconds or microseconds. Profiting from minor price differences in the market by taking advantage of pricing and liquidity inefficiencies is one of HFT's main goals.

Market making, where traders give the market liquidity by continuously quoting bid and ask prices for a specific asset, is one of the most popular HFT strategies. Market makers try to make a little profit on each trade that is executed by taking advantage of the difference between the ask and bid prices. Market makers assist in preserving orderly markets and facilitating effective price discovery by quoting prices on both sides of the market and dynamically modifying them based on market conditions. But there are risks associated with market making as well, like being vulnerable to unfavorable price fluctuations and possibly losing money if the market conditions change quickly.

Arbitrage is a different HFT strategy that involves taking advantage of price differences between various markets or trading venues. When an asset is trading at a different price in multiple markets, arbitrageurs can spot these instances and place trades to profit from the difference in price. Arbitrageurs, for instance, may profit from variations in exchange rates between currency pairs traded on various exchanges or liquidity providers in the forex market. Arbitrageurs can profit from these price differentials before the market corrects them by placing trades at a breakneck pace.

Another well-liked HFT tactic is statistical arbitrage, which entails spotting and taking advantage of trends or abnormalities in market data. Traders examine past price data, find connections between various assets, and forecast short-term price changes using statistical models and algorithms. Pairs trading, in which traders simultaneously purchase and sell two correlated assets in the hope that their prices will eventually converge, is a common component of statistical arbitrage strategies. Statistical arbitrageurs can profit by taking advantage of brief departures from their historical relationship while lowering their exposure to market risk.

Furthermore, a popular HFT strategy that takes advantage of the market's momentum and short-term price trends is momentum trading. In order to ride the trend and make quick profits, traders look for assets that are showing momentum or experiencing significant price movements. Traders using momentum trading strategies frequently engage in rapid-fire trading with high turnover rates, entering and exiting positions several times during the trading day. Momentum traders can profit from brief price changes and take advantage of market momentum by utilizing quickness and agility.

HFT strategies are widely used and popular, but their possible effects on market stability and fairness have drawn criticism. HFT companies' superior speed and technological capabilities, according to their detractors, could give them an unfair advantage over other market players and cause instability in the market. For instance, the fast-paced nature of HFT may intensify market turbulence and raise the possibility of flash crashes, in which prices fall sharply and unexpectedly. Concerns have also been expressed regarding how HFT may affect market liquidity and the reliability of price discovery processes.

In response to these worries, regulators have put policies in place to improve market transparency, keep an eye on HFT activity, and stop market manipulation. To deter excessive HFT activity, regulators might, for instance, impose minimum order resting times or charge fees for excessive order cancellations. In addition, circuit breakers and other safety measures have been put in place by exchanges and trading venues to stop wild price swings and keep the markets in order.

Finally, high-frequency trading strategies, which provide previously unheard-of speed, efficiency, and liquidity, have completely transformed the forex market and the financial markets in general. HFT companies can take advantage of market inefficiencies, execute trades at breakneck speed, and profit from short-term price disparities by utilizing cutting-edge technology and algorithms. HFT tactics do, however, come with some risks and difficulties, such as worries about regulatory oversight, market stability, and equity. In order to fully utilize HFT while minimizing its hazards, traders need to be aware of the workings of HFT strategies, put strong risk management procedures in place, and keep a close eye on market conditions.

Automated Trading Systems

Automated trading systems, sometimes referred to as algorithmic trading or black-box trading, have become extremely effective instruments for accurately and efficiently executing trades in financial markets, such as the forex market. These systems evaluate market data, spot trading opportunities, and automatically execute trades without requiring human input. They do this by using computer algorithms. Automated trading systems, which provide many benefits like speed, accuracy, and emotion-free decision-making, have completely changed the way that trading is done.

The capacity of automated trading systems to execute trades at speeds that greatly exceed those of human traders is one of its main advantages. In a split second, these systems can evaluate a tonne of market data, including volume, price movements, and other indicators, and then execute trades in line with their analysis. Often ahead of human traders, automated trading systems can profit from even the slightest price fluctuations in the market by utilizing co-location and high-speed connections to trading servers.

Furthermore, automated trading systems provide trade execution with unmatched accuracy and consistency. Automated systems only use predefined rules and algorithms to make decisions; human traders may be subject to emotions, biases, and mistakes. This removes the possibility of human error and guarantees that trades are carried out precisely and consistently in accordance with preset criteria. Because of this, automated trading systems can obediently follow risk management procedures and trading strategies, assisting traders in avoiding rash or emotional decisions.

Automated trading systems also have the benefit of being able to run continuously without requiring human oversight. These systems enable traders to take advantage of trading opportunities as they present themselves by keeping an eye on the market around-the-clock, seven days a week, across multiple time zones and trading sessions. In addition to ensuring that no trading opportunities are lost, this constant observation enables traders to respond swiftly to shifts in the market, breaking news, or releases of economic data.

Additionally, before implementing trading strategies in real-time trading, automated trading systems can evaluate their performance and optimize parameters through backtesting using historical data. This enables traders to assess how well their strategies work in different market environments, spot any potential flaws or areas for development, and make the required changes to improve results. Through the process of backtesting strategies, traders can enhance their trading systems' confidence and make better-informed choices regarding their trading strategy.

Automated trading systems have many benefits, but there are also some risks and difficulties that traders need to be aware of. The possibility of technical malfunctions or system bugs, which can cause unforeseen losses or trading interruptions, is one of the main risks. Problems like hardware malfunctions, software bugs, or connectivity issues can arise and result in orders being missed or traded incorrectly. Traders need to put strong risk management procedures in place and have backup plans ready to handle technical problems quickly in order to reduce this risk.

Furthermore, automated trading systems might be vulnerable to overfitting, a phenomenon in which trading strategies that are overly tuned to past data perform poorly in real-time trading. When a trading system is too complicated or has too many parameters, it is said to be overfitting. This means that it is unable to adjust to new or unseen data and is excessively sensitive to previous market conditions. Traders should utilize robust testing protocols, appropriate risk management strategies, and make sure their strategies are grounded in sound principles rather than arbitrary optimizations to prevent overfitting.

Furthermore, market conditions that vary from those experienced during back testing may expose automated trading systems to risk. Variations in market structure, liquidity, or volatility are a few examples of factors that can impact how well trading strategies perform in live trading. It is imperative for traders to consistently observe and assess the functioning of their automated systems, implementing modifications as needed to accommodate changing market circumstances and sustain profitability.

To sum up, automated trading systems have revolutionized the financial markets by providing faster, more accurate, and more efficient trading than human traders could ever hope to. These systems evaluate market data, spot trading opportunities, and automatically execute trades without requiring human intervention. They do this by utilizing cutting-edge technology and algorithms. Although automated trading systems have many benefits, such as speed, accuracy, and round-the-clock operation, there are also risks and difficulties associated with them that traders need to be aware of. Traders can maximize the benefits of automated trading systems while minimizing potential downsides and accomplishing their trading goals by being aware of these risks and putting strong risk management procedures in place.

Back testing and Optimization

Creating and improving trading strategies in financial markets, such as the forex market, requires the use of back testing and optimization. Back testing is evaluating a trading strategy's performance by simulating its performance in previous market conditions using historical market data. This enables traders to assess the performance of their strategies, pinpoint their advantages and disadvantages, and decide with confidence whether to use them in real-time trading. Through the process of back testing strategies, traders can obtain important insights into their past performance, comprehend their risk-reward profile, and improve their approach to improve their real-world trading results.

The capacity of back testing to offer unbiased, fact-based insights into the performance of trading strategies is one of its main advantages. Traders can evaluate how their strategies would have performed in different market conditions, such as different asset classes, time frames, and market environments, by running back tests using historical market data. Traders can improve their approach and trading decisions by using this empirical analysis to find patterns, correlations, and anomalies in their trading strategies.

Additionally, traders can evaluate the stability and dependability of their trading strategies under a variety of market conditions by using back testing. Traders can obtain a comprehensive understanding of their strategy's performance characteristics and its adaptability to changing market conditions by testing their strategies across a variety of market cycles, volatility regimes, and economic environments. This lowers the risk of overfitting and raises the possibility of success in live trading by assisting traders in identifying strategies that become more resilient and consistent over time.

Quantifying the risk-reward profile of trading strategies and evaluating their profitability potential are two more benefits of back testing. Traders can assess the overall performance of their strategies and ascertain whether they meet their profit objectives and risk tolerance by examining important performance metrics like profit and loss, win rate, maximum drawdown, and risk-adjusted returns. With the use of this quantitative analysis, traders can decide which strategies to use in real-time trading based on data, and they can allocate capital wisely in order to minimize risk and maximize returns.

Additionally, through back testing, traders can find areas where their trading strategies can be optimized and improved. Traders can determine areas in which their strategies may be underperforming or have room for improvement by examining the outcomes of back tests and performing sensitivity analyses on important parameters. To enhance performance, this can entail modifying the requirements for entry and exit, optimizing position sizing and risk management guidelines, or adding more indicators or filters. Traders can improve their strategies and adjust to changing market conditions by testing and optimizing them iteratively.

Back testing is a useful tool for assessing trading strategies, but traders need to be aware of its limitations and other factors. One drawback is the possibility of overfitting, in which trading strategies that are overly tailored to past data may not function well in real-time trading. Traders should utilize appropriate risk management strategies, robust testing protocols, and make sure their strategies are grounded in sound principles rather than arbitrary optimizations in order to reduce this risk.

Furthermore, market slippage, execution costs, and other real-world variables that can influence trading performance might not be completely captured by back testing. When interpreting the results of back tests, traders should take these factors into account and modify their expectations accordingly. Furthermore, before putting real money into a strategy, back testing ought to be combined with forward testing or paper trading to confirm the strategy's effectiveness in current market conditions.

To sum up, optimization and back testing are essential steps in the creation and improvement of trading strategies for the financial markets. Through the examination of past market data and the evaluation of strategy performance, traders can acquire important knowledge about the efficacy of their approach, spot areas for development, and refine their strategy to improve their live trading performance. Although back testing is an effective technique for strategy evaluation, traders should be aware of its drawbacks and limitations and combine it with forward testing to guarantee the stability and dependability of their trading systems.

CHAPTER VIII

Building a Forex Trading Plan

Setting Trading Goals

A crucial first step in becoming a profitable forex trader is setting trading objectives. Objectives offer guidance, inspiration, and a structure for assessing advancement and formulating well-informed choices. Achieving long-term success in the forex market requires setting specific, attainable goals, regardless of experience level. This applies to both novice and seasoned traders alike.

Setting goals for your trading starts with defining your objectives. What do you want to accomplish with forex trading? Do you want to improve your trading abilities, earn extra cash, or become financially independent? You can adjust your trading plan to match your unique goals and aspirations by making sure your objectives are clear.

The next stage after determining your goals is to create SMART goals, which stand for Specific, Measurable, Achievable, Relevant, and Time-bound. Well-defined objectives offer precision and concentration, allowing you to express exactly what you hope to achieve. Rather than aiming for a general objective such as "make more money," a more targeted one could be "achieve a monthly return of 5% on my trading account."

Measurable objectives enable you to monitor development and conduct an unbiased performance review. Clear success metrics, like win rates, profit targets, or risk-reward ratios, allow you to track your progress over time and make necessary corrections.

Within the limitations of your trading strategy, risk tolerance, and available resources, attainable goals are doable and feasible. Setting lofty objectives that push you to advance as a trader is great, but it's also critical to make sure that your goals are realistic given your current skill level and the state of the market.

Relevant goals are those that represent your distinct trading style, preferences, and personality while also being in line with your overall trading objectives. Your goals should be adjusted to allow for longer holding periods and a slower trading pace, for instance, if you prefer swing trading over day trading.

Lastly, time-bound objectives have a specified completion date or timeline. Setting deadlines for your trading goals instills a sense of accountability and urgency, which encourages you to take consistent action and stay on course to meet your goals.

Apart from establishing clear, quantifiable, attainable, pertinent, and time-bound objectives, it's crucial to rank them according to significance and exigency. Not every goal is the same, and achieving some may take more time, energy, and resources than others. You can increase your effectiveness and make significant progress toward your main goals by determining your top priorities and concentrating your efforts and attention on the most important tasks.

To make sure your trading objectives are still applicable and in line with your changing needs and circumstances, it's also critical to review and reevaluate them on a regular basis. Because the forex market is dynamic and constantly evolving, an objective that made sense yesterday might not make sense today. You can remain on course to achieve long-term success in forex trading and adjust to shifting market conditions by periodically reviewing and modifying your goals.

To sum up, the establishment of trading objectives is a fundamental phase in constructing an effective forex trading strategy. You can design a road map for success in the forex market by establishing specific objectives, prioritizing your goals, setting SMART goals, and routinely reviewing and reevaluating your goals. Realizing your full potential as a forex trader requires setting and pursuing meaningful goals, whether your objective is to increase your income, become financially independent, or simply become a better trader.

Choosing a Trading Style

For any forex trader, selecting a trading style is essential because it determines how you will approach the market, carry out trades, and handle risk. There are various trading philosophies to take into account, each with pros, cons, and suitability based on your personality, tastes, and trading objectives.

Day trading is a popular trading strategy where investors open and close positions within the same trading day in an effort to profit from transient price changes. Day traders need to be very focused, disciplined, and fast-thinking because they have to make decisions quickly and adjust to shifting market conditions. Even though day trading has the potential to be thrilling and profitable, there are risks involved, such as higher transaction costs and increased volatility.

Swing trading is another well-liked trading strategy that entails maintaining positions for a few days to a few weeks in order to profit from medium-term price trends. Swing traders use technical analysis and chart patterns to determine entry and exit points as they attempt to profit from price fluctuations within the larger market trends. Swing trading is appropriate for traders who prefer a slower trading pace and can tolerate overnight risk because it provides a balance between the longer-term perspective of position trading and the fast-paced nature of day trading.

Conversely, position trading entails maintaining positions for several weeks or months in order to profit from notable long-term price movements. Position traders often take a more comprehensive approach to the market and place a premium on patience and discipline. They base their trading decisions on fundamental analysis and macroeconomic trends. Position trading calls for a longer-term commitment and the capacity to tolerate brief price swings in the market, even though it takes less time and effort than swing or day trading.

Another trading strategy is called scalping, which is defined by making a lot of trades quickly with the goal of making money off of slight price changes. In order to find short-term trading opportunities, scalpers usually concentrate on the currency pairs that are the most liquid. They use technical indicators like moving averages and support and resistance levels. Scalping can be extremely profitable for experienced traders, but in order to minimize the high transaction costs and possible losses connected with frequent trading, scalping demands lightning-fast reflexes, cutting-edge trading technology, and stringent risk management.

In the end, your trading style selection is influenced by a number of variables, such as your trading goals, personality, lifestyle, and risk tolerance. While some traders may thrive in the fast-paced world of day trading, others might favor swing trading's more laid-back style or position trading's methodical discipline. Before choosing a trading style, it's critical to honestly evaluate your advantages and disadvantages, take into account the time and resources you have available, and carefully consider the advantages and disadvantages of each trading style.

Furthermore, it's critical to keep in mind that your trading style is flexible and may change as you develop experience and improve your approach. It's important to find a trading style that complements your own strengths, preferences, and objectives because what works for one trader might not be suitable for another. You can create a customized trading strategy that increases your chances of success in the forex market by experimenting with various trading philosophies, getting advice from more seasoned traders, and continually learning about and adjusting to market conditions.

To sum up, selecting a trading style is an essential step in creating a forex trading plan and necessitates giving careful thought to a number of variables, such as your personality, lifestyle, risk tolerance, and trading goals. There is a trading style to fit every trader, whether they favor the fast-paced action of day trading, the medium-term outlook of swing trading, the patient discipline of position trading, or the lightning-fast precision of scalping. In the dynamic and constantly changing world of forex trading, you can improve your chances of success and reach your trading objectives by choosing a style that complements your preferences and strong points and by continuously improving your strategy through practice and experience.

Creating and Evaluating a Trading Plan

In order to successfully navigate the market's complexities and meet their trading objectives, forex traders must develop and assess a trading plan. A trading plan outlines your trading goals, tactics, and risk control procedures. It functions as a road map. It gives you consistency, discipline, and structure so you can confidently manage your trades and make well-informed decisions. However, developing a strong trading plan necessitates giving careful thought to a number of variables, such as market analysis, risk assessment, and performance evaluation.

Identifying your goals and defining your objectives are the first steps in developing a trading plan. What do you want to accomplish with forex trading? Are you trying to become financially independent, make extra money, or just get better at trading? You can customize your trading plan to fit your own goals and circumstances by defining your objectives and establishing attainable goals.

The next step after deciding on your aims and objectives is to create a trading plan that is supported by in-depth market research and analysis. This include defining risk management parameters, identifying high-probability trading setups, and figuring out entry and exit points. Selecting a trading strategy that aligns with your trading style, inclinations, and risk tolerance is essential, regardless of whether you favor technical analysis, fundamental analysis, or a blend of both.

Any trading plan must include risk management, which entails identifying and reducing possible risks in order to safeguard your investment and maintain profitability. This entails defining position sizes according to your account size and risk tolerance, setting stop-loss orders, and diversifying your trades to spread risk across various asset classes or currency pairs. Strong risk management procedures can help you reduce the effects of unfavorable market movements and make sure your trading strategy is viable over the long run.

It's critical to continuously assess and improve your trading plan in light of your performance and the state of the market after you've created it. This entails monitoring important performance indicators and pinpointing areas in need of development, such as win percentage, average profit and loss, and risk-reward ratio. You can find the strengths and weaknesses in your trading plan and make the necessary adjustments to improve your overall performance by going over your trades and evaluating your results objectively.

It's critical to assess your trading plan not only on the basis of performance metrics but also taking into account external factors like shifts in market dynamics, economic indicators, and geopolitical developments. Because the forex market is dynamic and constantly shifting, strategies that were effective yesterday might not be as effective tomorrow. You can make sure that your trading plan stays relevant and successful over time by keeping yourself informed and making adjustments to reflect changing market conditions.

Furthermore, it's critical to stick to your trading plan with consistency and discipline even in the face of obstacles or failures. Fear, greed, and overconfidence are examples of emotions that can impair judgment and cause impulsive decisions that are detrimental to your trading strategy. You can get over psychological obstacles and continue to trade in a logical, disciplined manner by following your set rules and procedures.

To sum up, developing and assessing a trading plan is crucial for forex traders to be successful in the fast-paced, cutthroat world of currency trading. You can improve your chances of success and reach your trading objectives by setting clear goals, creating a solid trading strategy, putting in place efficient risk management procedures, and routinely reviewing and adjusting your plan in light of performance and market conditions. There is no one-size-fits-all method for successful trading, but you can overcome the challenges of the foreign exchange market and turn a profit over the long run by creating a customized trading plan that plays to your strengths, preferences, and goals.

Adjusting Strategies Based on Market Conditions

Success in the dynamic and constantly shifting world of forex trading requires the ability to modify strategies in response to market conditions. The state of the market can fluctuate greatly, from times of low volatility and range-bound price action to times of high volatility and swift price movements. In order to take advantage of opportunities and reduce risks, traders must be able to identify when market conditions are changing and modify their strategies accordingly.

Changing the duration of your trades in accordance with the state of the market is one frequent strategy adjustment. Shorter time frames, like intraday or scalping strategies, may be more appropriate during times of high volatility and rapid price movements. This allows traders to profit from short-term price fluctuations and momentum-driven moves. On the other hand, longer time frames, like swing trading or position trading strategies, may be more successful during times of low volatility and range-bound price action. These strategies allow traders to capture larger price movements within the framework of more general market trends.

Depending on the state of the market, another strategy adjustment is to move the emphasis from technical analysis to fundamental analysis or the other way around. Fundamental analysis can offer useful insights into market sentiment and direction during times of increased uncertainty or noteworthy macroeconomic events. This enables traders to make well-informed trading decisions based on economic indicators, central bank policies, and geopolitical developments. On the other hand, technical analysis may be more trustworthy when price action is dominated by technical factors or when market conditions are stable. This is because it helps traders make trading decisions by helping them recognize important levels of support and resistance, trend patterns, and chart formations.

Another essential component of modifying strategies in response to market conditions is risk management. Tightening risk management procedures and reducing position sizes are crucial during times of increased volatility or uncertainty in order to safeguard capital and maintain profitability. This could be increasing stop-loss orders, lowering leverage, or even withdrawing from the market for a while until things settle down. On the other hand, traders may think about leveraging up or taking on larger positions in times of low volatility or when trading in well-established trends in order to take advantage of advantageous risk-reward opportunities.

Furthermore, constant observation and analysis of important indicators and market drivers is necessary to remain informed and adjust to changing market conditions. This could entail keeping up with news from the central bank, economic releases, geopolitical events, and other sources that could affect market sentiment and currency values. Traders can spot new trends and opportunities and modify their strategies to stay ahead of the curve by being proactive and watchful when evaluating the state of the market.

In conclusion, a key component of creating a profitable forex trading plan is modifying strategies in response to market conditions. In the dynamic and constantly shifting world of currency trading, you can take advantage of opportunities, reduce risks, and preserve a competitive edge by identifying when market conditions are changing and adjusting your strategies accordingly. The ability to adapt strategies based on market conditions is crucial for navigating the complexities of the forex market and achieving long-term profitability. This includes changing time frames, focusing on technical rather than fundamental analysis, adjusting risk management protocols, and remaining informed and proactive in monitoring market developments.

CHAPTER IX

Reviewing Forex Brokerage Options

Types of Forex Brokers

By giving traders access to currency pairs and execution platforms, forex brokers are essential in enabling trading activities in the foreign exchange market. Understanding the various broker types and their unique features, offerings, and cost structures is crucial when thinking about forex brokerage options. Market makers, brokers using the electronic communication network (ECN), and brokers using direct market access (DMA) are the three primary categories into which forex brokers fall.

Dealing desk brokers, or market makers, take the other side of a trade in order to facilitate execution by acting as counterparties to the trades of their clients. The two prices that market makers usually quote are the ask price, which they are willing to sell to the trader, and the bid price, at which they are willing to purchase a currency pair from the trader. The spread, or the price difference between the ask and bid, is how market makers get paid. Market makers may have conflicts of interest because they benefit when traders lose money, even though they provide liquidity and convenience. Furthermore, market makers might partake in actions like slippage or requoting, which could lower the quality of trade execution.

ECN brokers act as middlemen, connecting their clients' buy and sell orders with market counterparties. Instead of taking the opposite position in their clients' trades as market makers do, ECN brokers route orders through to liquidity providers like banks, financial institutions, and other traders. Because ECN brokers aggregate prices from multiple liquidity providers and pass on the best available prices to their clients, they typically offer tighter spreads and more transparent pricing. ECN brokers may also provide features like direct market access (DMA) and depth of market (DOM) data, which let traders view real-time order book information and obtain liquidity directly.

DMA brokers eliminate middlemen like market makers and ECN brokers by giving traders direct access to the interbank foreign exchange market. DMA brokers give traders direct market access to liquidity providers, allowing them to access deeper liquidity pools and execute trades at the best prices. In addition to spreads, DMA brokers usually charge a commission for their services, but they also provide more transparent pricing and quicker execution times. DMA brokers may also provide sophisticated trading tools and features like customizable order types, algorithmic trading, and institutional-grade liquidity.

It is important to take into account various aspects when selecting a forex broker, including security, customer support, trading platforms, regulation, and pricing. The integrity of the market and the safety of client funds depend heavily on regulatory oversight. The Australian Securities and Investments Commission (ASIC), the UK Financial Conduct Authority (FCA), the US Commodity Futures Trading Commission (CFTC), and the European Securities and Markets Authority (ESMA) are examples of credible regulatory organizations.

Cyber threats and unauthorized access can be warded off with the aid of security measures like two-factor authentication (2FA), segregated client funds, and encryption protocols. Furthermore, the broker's trading platform ought to be easy to use, reliable, and furnished with fundamental features like order management, technical indicators, and charting tools. For problems to be addressed and questions to be answered quickly, customer service must be dependable, especially when there is market volatility or technical difficulties.

Different forex brokers have different pricing structures, which can have a big impact on trading expenses and earnings. Some brokers charge a commission but provide tighter spreads and more transparent pricing, while others offer commission-free trading with wider spreads. The total cost of trading should be carefully considered by traders, accounting for spreads, commissions, overnight financing fees, and any other relevant expenses.

In summary, it is critical to comprehend the various categories of forex brokers and their attributes in order to choose a brokerage partner with confidence. Based on your needs, preferences, and trading style, you can select a market maker, ECN broker, or DMA broker. You can select a broker who satisfies your requirements and offers a dependable and transparent trading environment for carrying out your forex strategies by taking into account variables like regulation, security, trading platforms, customer support, and pricing.

Factors to Consider When Choosing a Broker

Within the vast realm of foreign exchange trading, choosing the best brokerage is akin to building a strong and successful trading journey. This process of making decisions requires a careful analysis of many important variables, each of which has a unique bearing on how trading activities develop. The most important of these factors is regulatory compliance, which is a non-negotiable cornerstone that ensures the security and integrity of trading operations. Choosing a broker who is governed by a respectable financial regulator not only provides traders with a safe haven for their money, but it also inspires confidence as long as the industry norms are followed. In the event of disagreements or anomalies, regulatory supervision serves as a crucial safeguard against possible malpractices and gives traders a vital avenue for resolution. In order to safeguard investors' interests and guarantee honest and open trading practices, regulatory organizations like the Financial Conduct Authority (FCA) in the UK and the Securities and Exchange Commission (SEC) in the US impose stringent rules and regulations on brokers.

Another essential component of the broker selection procedure is transparency. Traders need to look for brokers that have clear fee schedules, free of any extra expenses that might eventually eat away at profits. Transparency should encompass the broker's policies regarding slippage, requotes, and other possible sources of hidden charges, in addition to the transactional costs that are readily visible. In addition to assisting traders in efficiently managing their expenses, having a thorough understanding of all fees and charges related to trading promotes openness and trust in the broker-client relationship. Furthermore, the level of execution quality provided by the broker is extremely important. Order execution must be quick and accurate, as inefficiencies or delays can jeopardize even the most carefully thought out trading plans. Thus, in order to maximize trading effectiveness and efficiency, choose a broker who has a reputation for being adept at timely and precise trade execution. It's wise for traders to investigate and contrast execution times and dependability amongst brokers to make sure they choose a platform that fits their trading preferences and style.

Because the trading platform serves as a major entry point to the forex market, traders place a high value on its usability and functionality. Trading experiences can be greatly improved by a platform that is easy to use and has strong features for order management and technical analysis. Moreover, the platform's compatibility with a wide range of hardware and operating systems guarantees smooth access, enabling traders to access the market from any location or on their preferred device. The trading environment has undergone even more revolution with the rise of mobile trading apps, which allow traders to manage their portfolios, execute trades, and access real-time market data while on the go. Even though many traders still prioritize forex, there are other tradable instruments that are worth taking into account. Brokers that provide access to other markets—like stocks, commodities, and cryptocurrencies—offer traders the chance to diversify their holdings and accommodate a range of trading philosophies and tactics.

Cost factors include the broker's leverage offerings in addition to spreads and commissions. Although using a lot of leverage can increase profits, it also increases risk exposure. Traders must find a careful balance between risk management and cost efficiency. Furthermore, traders' overall experiences can be significantly impacted by the caliber of customer service. Help that is both knowledgeable and timely is very important, especially when there are urgent questions or technical difficulties. Therefore, choosing a broker that places a high priority on accessible and dependable customer service channels is crucial to ensuring a smooth trading experience.

Broker educational materials are incredibly helpful, especially for traders who want to increase their expertise. Having access to webinars, tutorials, and market analyses can help traders gain a better understanding of the dynamics of the forex market, enabling them to hone their tactics and make wise choices. Furthermore, one should not undervalue a broker's reputation or track record. Testimonials from other traders, awards from the industry, and the broker's length of time in the business offer important clues about its dependability and legitimacy.

Finally, practical factors like the effectiveness and accessibility of deposit and withdrawal options complete the broker selection procedure. A broker that provides a range of safe and practical ways to make payments guarantees smooth transactions, reducing the amount of administrative work and promoting more efficient trading operations. In summary, choosing the best forex broker requires a thorough assessment of a number of variables. In the dynamic world of forex trading, a trader's experiences and results are shaped by a variety of factors, including regulatory compliance, transparency, the quality of the trading platform, the diversity of instruments, costs, customer support, educational resources, reputation, and payment options. Traders can make well-informed decisions and position themselves for success in navigating the complexities of the forex market landscape by carefully considering these factors.

Evaluation of Brokerage Platforms

Choosing the appropriate brokerage platform is crucial for traders who want to successfully negotiate the intricacies of the foreign exchange market. A number of important factors are taken into consideration when evaluating brokerage platforms, including customer service, trading tools, security protocols, and regulatory compliance. Regulatory supervision is an essential factor to consider when evaluating brokerage platforms. Traders need to make sure that a broker is subject to regulation by respectable organizations like the UK Financial Conduct Authority (FCA) or the US Securities and Exchange Commission (SEC). Traders can feel more secure knowing that their broker is following industry norms and regulations thanks to regulatory compliance, which also protects their money from dishonesty and misconduct.

An additional important consideration when assessing brokerage platforms is security measures. In order to protect confidential client information and safeguard sensitive financial data, traders should give preference to platforms that use strong encryption technologies. Furthermore, multi-factor authentication techniques strengthen the security framework even more by preventing unauthorized access to trading accounts and lowering the dangers brought on by cyberattacks. Traders are more confident when using a secure brokerage platform, which creates a favorable atmosphere for placing trades and managing investment portfolios without worrying about identity theft or data breaches.

A brokerage platform's features and functionality have a big impact on whether or not traders will find it suitable, even outside of compliance with regulations and security measures. The trading experience is improved by an intuitive and user-friendly interface, which makes it easier to navigate between different trading instruments and analytical tools. Traders are enabled to make well-informed decisions and profit from profitable trading opportunities by means of sophisticated charting capabilities, real-time market data, and customizable trading indicators. Additionally, having access to a wide variety of trading instruments, such as indices, commodities, and major currency pairs, allows traders to diversify their holdings and maximize returns after accounting for risk.

Cutting-edge trading tools and technologies are essential for setting brokerage platforms apart and strengthening their competitive advantage. In the forex market, automated trading algorithms—also referred to as expert advisors, or EAs—allow traders to carry out predetermined trading strategies precisely and effectively, removing human error and emotional bias from the decision-making process. Social trading platforms also help traders collaborate and share knowledge, which enables newcomers to replicate the trading strategies of experienced professionals and shortens their learning curve in the forex market.

Successful forex trading requires effective risk management, which emphasizes the value of the analytical tools and risk assessment processes provided by brokerage platforms. Risk calculators, margin requirements, and stop-loss orders enable traders to create sensible risk management plans and reduce possible losses in erratic market circumstances. Furthermore, brokerage platforms offer traders the knowledge and insights required to navigate dynamic market trends and modify their trading strategies, thanks to their extensive educational resources and market analysis materials.

When it comes to customer support, prompt and informed assistance is essential to answering traders' questions and fixing technical problems. Brokerage platforms that provide multilingual support channels—such as email, phone, and live chat—address the various demands of their global clientele, cultivating enduring client relationships and augmenting user contentment. Additionally, traders are empowered to fully utilize the brokerage platform and improve their trading performance over time thanks to informative webinars, tutorials, and FAQ sections.

To sum up, the review of brokerage platforms includes an extensive analysis of features related to risk management, trading functionality, security protocols, creative tools, and regulatory compliance. By giving priority to these important factors, traders can find brokerage platforms that fit their trading goals, risk appetite, and personal preferences; this will set them up for success and happiness as they navigate the ever-changing world of forex trading.

Account Management and Support Services

The foundations of the forex trading industry are account management and support services, which provide traders with crucial direction and aid as they negotiate the complexities of financial markets. These services cover a wide range of products and services that are designed to make transactions easy, control risk well, and maximize trading performance in order to meet financial goals. Effective trade execution on behalf of clients is the foundation of account management. Forex brokers make use of sophisticated trading platforms that have lightning-fast order execution capabilities to guarantee that trades are completed accurately and on time, allowing traders to seize short-lived market opportunities right away. Additionally, account managers frequently offer customized trading recommendations and advice based on each client's particular risk tolerance and investing goals, assisting them in reaching their financial objectives.

Robust risk management strategies are essential to account management services, and they also help with trade execution. Account managers work closely with customers to create thorough risk management strategies that guard trading money and reduce possible losses. These plans frequently include a range of risk-reduction tactics, including well-placed stop-loss orders, methodical position-sizing plans, and prudent portfolio diversification techniques. Account managers enable traders to confidently navigate volatile market conditions by putting prudent risk management practices into place. This protects traders' investment portfolios from excessive volatility and helps to preserve capital over the long run

.

Effective account management also includes portfolio analysis and performance assessment in addition to trade execution and risk management. Account managers perform comprehensive evaluations of their clients' investment portfolios, pinpointing areas of strength, weakness, and potential improvement by utilizing advanced analytical tools and techniques. Account managers help clients fine-tune their approaches to maximize returns and minimize risks by offering insightful information on the effectiveness of trading strategies through routine portfolio reviews and performance reports. Account managers can also provide clients with tailored investment solutions and advice on asset allocation based on their risk tolerance and the state of the market. This allows clients to diversify their holdings and take advantage of new opportunities across a range of asset classes.

Robust support infrastructure is necessary to ensure a smooth trading experience and promptly respond to clients' questions and concerns, especially when combined with account management services. Forex brokers normally provide a multitude of customer service channels, such as live chat, email, and phone support, all of which are manned by competent and helpful customer service agents. Quick resolution of technical problems, account-related questions, and trading concerns builds strong client-broker relationships based on trust and dependability and increases clients' confidence in the brokerage platform. Moreover, multilingual support services meet the varied demands of a global clientele and enable traders globally to communicate and receive assistance in a variety of languages and time zones.

Comprehensive educational materials and training programs are essential parts of the support services offered by forex brokers, in addition to prompt customer service. Brokerage firms provide a multitude of educational resources, covering a wide range of subjects like technical analysis, fundamental analysis, risk management strategies, and forex trading strategies. These resources include interactive webinars, educational tutorials, perceptive articles, and comprehensive trading guides. Furthermore, demo accounts are very helpful for new traders because they let them practice trading in a virtual setting without having to risk real money. This helps them improve their skills and become more familiar with the workings of the trading platform.

Forex brokers enable their clients to make well-informed trading decisions and confidently and competently navigate the volatile and competitive forex market by investing in trader education and skill development. To sum up, account management and support services are essential parts of the ecosystem surrounding forex brokerages because they give traders the direction, help, and tools they need to reach their financial goals. Forex brokers enable their clients to trade with confidence and achieve long-term success by providing them with a seamless experience through effective trade execution, strong risk management, perceptive portfolio analysis, and attentive customer support. Trading professionals can collaborate with brokerage firms that provide the know-how, dependability, and assistance required for success in the ever-changing forex market by giving account management and support services top priority.

CHAPTER X

Real-World Case Studies

Successful Forex Trading Stories

of navigating the volatile and frequently unpredictable currency markets are common in the world of foreign exchange trading. Aspiring traders can gain inspiration from these success stories, which provide insightful information about the tactics, perseverance, and mindset needed to achieve long-term success in forex trading. George Soros is a prime example of this; his trade in 1992 was so spectacular that it made him the man known as "The Man Who Broke the Bank of England." Famously, Soros wagered against the British pound, expecting economic pressures within the European Exchange Rate Mechanism to eventually cause its devaluation. Soros profited from the pound's decline by short-selling billions of pounds sterling; in one day, he reportedly made over $1 billion in profits. His reputation as one of the most successful forex traders of all time was cemented by his astute analysis and decisive action.

Stanley Druckenmiller, a former colleague of George Soros at Quantum Fund, is another noteworthy success story. In carrying out the well-known deal that resulted in the devaluation of the British pound in 1992, Druckenmiller was a key player. He made significant profits from the trade and solidified his status as a top forex trader thanks to his astute observations of macroeconomic trends and his ability to spot high-probability trading opportunities. Druckenmiller's long-term success in forex trading has been largely attributed to his strict approach to risk management and his openness to adjust to shifting market conditions.

Apart from prominent institutional traders such as Soros and Druckenmiller, a multitude of individual traders have attained notable success in foreign exchange trading by virtue of their commitment, diligence, and astute analysis of market dynamics. Linda Bradford Raschke, a well-known trader and author recognized for her proficiency in short-term trading strategies, is one such trader. Raschke began her career as a floor trader on the Pacific Coast Stock Exchange in the 1980s, and that is how her path to success in forex trading began. Raschke refined her trading techniques and created a distinct trading strategy based on technical analysis and market psychology over the years. Raschke's success story has inspired many traders worldwide, as she has consistently achieved profitability in forex trading through her disciplined approach and unwavering pursuit of excellence.

Bill Lipschutz, a former foreign exchange trader at Salomon Brothers and one of the most successful traders in history, is another inspirational success story. During his tenure at Salomon Brothers, Lipschutz swiftly advanced through the ranks to assume leadership of the forex trading desk, marking the beginning of his successful career in forex trading. Lipschutz gained a reputation as one of Wall Street's top forex traders thanks to his skillful trading and ability to take advantage of market inefficiencies, which allowed him to produce large profits for the company. After leaving Salomon Brothers, Lipschutz founded Hathersage Capital Management, where he used his methodical approach and astute comprehension of market dynamics to continue his incredible success in forex trading.

The varied routes to success in forex trading are highlighted by the achievements of traders such as Bill Lipschutz, Linda Bradford Raschke, George Soros, and Stanley Druckenmiller. These traders have different histories, trading philosophies, and approaches, but they all possess qualities like self-control, endurance, and an unwavering quest of greatness. Their experiences serve as potent reminders that anyone who is prepared to work hard, hone their skills, and adjust to shifting market conditions can succeed in forex trading. Aspiring forex traders can learn a great deal about the mindset and tactics needed to succeed long-term in the fast-paced, cutthroat world of forex trading by examining the triumphs and setbacks of these renowned traders.

Analysis of Winning Trades

Analyzing profitable trades is a key component in comprehending the dynamics that propel success in the world of financial markets. By carefully analyzing and considering trades that have produced profitable results, traders and investors can obtain important insights into the tactics, methods, and market circumstances that are favorable to success. This kind of analysis not only acknowledges accomplishments but also provides a guide for improving decision-making in the future and optimizing returns.

Examining the underlying causes of successful trades is one of the main components of winning trade analysis. A number of components are covered in this analysis, such as technical indicators, market trends, fundamental analysis, and risk management techniques. Through examining these elements, traders hope to identify trends and connections that they can use to their advantage in future transactions. For example, traders can be better equipped to take advantage of similar opportunities in the future if they can spot a recurring pattern in price movements or determine how certain economic indicators affect asset prices.

Furthermore, the examination of profitable trades goes beyond determining profit margins; it also includes a thorough evaluation of risk-adjusted returns. As desirable as it Is to realize sizable gains, it is just as important to assess the risk exposure involved in each trade. Traders can determine whether the returns obtained are sufficient to offset the amount of risk they have taken by looking at metrics like the Sharpe ratio. Maintaining a stable and well-balanced trading portfolio, averting possible losses, and long-term capital preservation all depend on this risk-return analysis.

Moreover, examining profitable trades provides a chance for reflection and personal development. Prosperous traders understand the importance of ongoing education and strategy improvement. Traders can pinpoint their areas of strength and room for improvement in their trading strategy by closely examining previous victories. This procedure could entail optimizing entry and exit points, modifying the size of positions, or improving risk management procedures. By means of iterative self-evaluation and adjustment, traders can improve their competency and adaptability in maneuvering through the ever-changing financial markets.

An essential component of evaluating profitable trades is placing them in the context of larger market and macroeconomic trends. Numerous factors, such as geopolitical developments, central bank policies, and international economic indicators, have an impact on markets. Through the analysis of how profitable trades correlate with overall market sentiment and macroeconomic patterns, traders can acquire a more profound understanding of the fundamental factors that propel their success. This macro view improves comprehension and makes it easier to make well-informed decisions in advance of future market developments.

Moreover, the examination of profitable transactions provides a basis for developing strong trading frameworks and strategies. Traders can create systematic approaches and rule-based methodologies to direct their trading activities in the future by extracting important lessons from previous successes. Trading hypotheses can be validated and refined through empirical evidence obtained from the analysis of profitable trades, regardless of whether the strategies employed are trend-following, mean reversion, or volatility-based models. This evidence-based strategy encourages consistency and discipline in trading execution, which eventually produces more repeatable and predictable results.

Furthermore, traders can develop a resilient and adaptable mindset in the face of difficulty by studying profitable trades. Although confidence grows with success, traders will inevitably experience downturns and losses. Traders can gain strength from their past triumphs and learn how to overcome obstacles and recover from setbacks when facing difficult times. This psychological toughness plays a crucial role in preserving discipline and composure in tumultuous market conditions, enabling traders to remain committed to their long-term goals.

To sum up, analyzing profitable trades is a complex process that goes beyond just making money. It involves a careful analysis of the variables that influence success, a strict evaluation of risk-adjusted returns, and a dedication to lifelong learning and personal development. Through placing profitable trades in the context of larger market trends and macroeconomic circumstances, traders can better understand the dynamics that underpin their success. Furthermore, the examination of profitable trades is essential for developing strong trading plans, encouraging self-control, and developing a resilient and adaptive mindset. Because of this, it continues to be a vital tool in the toolbox of any profitable trader, directing their decision-making and forming their path to financial success.

Lessons Learned from Failed Trades

Failed trades are powerful teaching tools in the volatile world of financial markets, providing priceless insights into the complexities of trading and investing. Traders will always experience losses and setbacks while navigating the complex dynamics of the market; every loss and setback has lessons to be learned. Examining the elements that led to a trade's failure requires a thorough analysis of the market, risk management, decision-making processes, and psychological variables, among other things. Through a rigorous and introspective analysis of these losses, traders can draw important lessons that help them in their future trading endeavors and strengthen their ability to overcome obstacles.

The value of careful market research and due diligence is one of the main things that can be taken away from unsuccessful trades. In retrospect, poor research or a misreading of market trends can be held responsible for a great deal of unsuccessful trades. Traders might have underestimated the influence of macroeconomic factors on asset prices, missed important information, or failed to foresee unforeseen events. Traders can gain a more sophisticated understanding of market dynamics and make more thoughtful and informed trading decisions by realizing the importance of thorough market analysis.

Failed trades also highlight how crucial it is to implement efficient risk management techniques. Capital preservation and loss mitigation must always come first for traders in their quest of profit. Inadequate risk management procedures can put traders at unnecessary risk and make negative market movements more severe. Efficient risk management techniques, such as placing stop-loss orders, diversifying holdings, and adhering to pre-established risk-reward ratios, are essential for preventing catastrophic losses and extending stock market careers.

Furthermore, dissecting unsuccessful trades illuminates the influence of psychological elements on trading results. Trading performance can be severely hampered by emotions like fear, greed, and overconfidence, which can impair judgment and cause irrational decision-making. Trade failures are frequently painful reminders of the dangers of giving in to your emotions and straying from disciplined trading methods. Trading professionals can lessen the negative effects of psychological biases and keep a cool, collected head when faced with market swings by developing self-awareness and emotional resilience.

The significance of flexibility and adaptation in trading strategies is further highlighted by unsuccessful trades. Markets are dynamic and constantly changing, with sentiment, volatility, and liquidity all changing all the time. It's not a given that what has succeeded in the past will do so again. Traders need to be open to reevaluating their plans, making adjustments when needed, and embracing creativity and experimentation. Trade failures give traders insightful feedback that helps them improve their strategies, investigate new avenues, and adjust to shifting market conditions—all of which help them become more versatile and adaptive traders.

Failed trades are also humbling experiences that help traders become more resilient and humble. When one fails, it's easy to give in to doubt and hopelessness. Resilient traders, on the other hand, see failure as a chance for personal development. They approach every setback with an attitude of inquiry and reflection, looking to identify the underlying reasons behind their mistakes and derive useful lessons for the future. Through accepting failure as an inevitable part of the trading journey, traders develop a resilience and humility that helps them overcome obstacles and setbacks in the future.

To sum up, the examination of unsuccessful transactions provides a plethora of insights that significantly influence the growth and prosperity of traders. Failed trades offer a rich tapestry of experiences from which traders can learn and develop, from the significance of careful market analysis and effective risk management to the role of psychological factors and the necessity of adaptability. Traders can turn losses into opportunities and confidently and skillfully negotiate the volatile financial markets by embracing failure with humility, perseverance, and a dedication to ongoing improvement. As a result, losing trades are both a lesson learned and a means of improving one's trading skills and performance.

Applying Strategies to Real Market Scenarios

The application of trading strategies to real-world scenarios is a formidable challenge and a crucial factor in determining success in the volatile and dynamic world of financial markets. The effectiveness of trading strategies in actual market conditions is contingent upon various factors, such as investor sentiment, market dynamics, geopolitical events, and economic indicators, even though they have been carefully designed and thoroughly tested in controlled settings. Because of this, traders need to be flexible and able to see ahead in order to convert their strategies into decisions that can be implemented and that fit current market conditions and trends.

The identification of market inefficiencies and opportunities is a basic principle in the application of trading strategies to actual market situations. Inefficiencies in the financial markets are caused by things like asymmetrical information, herd mentality, and illogical investor sentiment. Proficient traders are able to recognize these inefficiencies and take advantage of them. Whether it's taking advantage of undervalued assets, arbitraging differences between similar instruments, or making money from market anomalies, traders need to have an acute sense of what opportunities others might miss.

Furthermore, a deep comprehension of macroeconomic trends and market dynamics is required in order to apply trading strategies to actual market scenarios. Numerous factors, such as central bank policies, geopolitical tensions, economic data releases, and world events, have an impact on markets. It is imperative for traders to remain updated about these developments and evaluate their possible effects on asset values and market sentiment. Traders can make more informed and sophisticated decisions based on a thorough understanding of the fundamental forces driving market movements by placing their trading strategies within the larger market trends and themes.

Furthermore, careful execution and risk management are necessary for the successful application of trading strategies to actual market situations. Even though trading strategies might seem like a surefire way to make money, not every trade will end up profitable. To lessen the impact of losses, traders need to be ready to accept them and follow risk management procedures. This could entail following predetermined risk-reward ratios, diversifying portfolios, or placing stop-loss orders. Traders can safeguard their capital and extend their market longevity by upholding discipline and practicing good risk management.

Additionally, flexibility and adaptability are required when applying trading strategies to actual market situations. Markets are dynamic and constantly changing, with volatility, liquidity, and investor sentiment all changing all the time. It's not a given that what has succeeded in the past will do so again. Traders need to be prepared to review their plans, change course when needed, and adjust to shifting market circumstances. This could entail modifying position sizing, adjusting parameters, or investigating completely different strategies. Traders can stay ahead of the curve and profit from newly emerging opportunities in the market by continuing to be adaptable and open-minded.

Furthermore, persistence and patience are necessary for the effective application of trading strategies to actual market situations. It is easy for traders to give in to emotional impulses and stray from their trading plans when faced with uncertainty and volatility. Resilient traders, on the other hand, remain calm and disciplined, adhering to their plans despite hardship. They are aware that the consistency and discipline with which they carry out their trading strategies over an extended period of time, rather than any one trade, determines their level of success. Traders can weather market ups and downs and emerge stronger and more skilled in their trade by developing patience and resilience.

Finally, it should be noted that applying trading strategies to actual market situations is a complex process that calls for flexibility, foresight, discipline, and resilience. Ability to recognize opportunities and inefficiencies in the market, comprehend macroeconomic and market dynamics, execute trades with discipline and risk management, and patiently and resiliently adjust to shifting market conditions are all characteristics of successful traders. By developing these abilities, traders can attain their trading objectives and financial goals by confidently and skillfully navigating the complex financial markets. Because of this, applying trading strategies to actual market situations continues to be a difficult task. .

CHAPTER XI

Future Trends in Forex Trading

Technological Innovations in Forex Markets

Technological innovations are bringing in a new era of efficiency, transparency, and accessibility in the forex trading industry, constantly changing the landscape. These developments cover a broad spectrum of fields, including blockchain technology, artificial intelligence, and the automation of trading procedures. Every new development has the potential to completely change how traders interact with the foreign exchange markets by providing them with fresh resources and perspectives on how to handle the challenges involved in currency trading.

The emergence of algorithmic trading has been one of the most revolutionary technological developments in forex trading. Algorithmic trading, sometimes referred to as automated or black-box trading, is the automation of trade execution through the use of computer algorithms that operate according to predetermined parameters. These parameters could be signals of market sentiment, price levels, or technical indicators. Traders can take advantage of short-lived opportunities and execute trades with unmatched efficiency thanks to algorithmic trading, which leverages the speed and accuracy of computers. Furthermore, real-time analysis of enormous volumes of data by algorithmic trading algorithms can reveal patterns and correlations that human traders might miss, improving trading profitability and performance.

Furthermore, the use of machine learning and artificial intelligence (AI) in forex trading is growing. Massive datasets can be analyzed by AI algorithms with previously unheard-of speed and accuracy, revealing hidden patterns and trends that affect currency prices. By using AI-driven models in their trading strategies, traders can make better, more data-driven decisions, giving them a competitive advantage. Furthermore, trading systems driven by AI have the capacity to adjust and develop over time, continuously gaining new insights from data and honing their tactics to maximize performance in shifting market circumstances.

The application of blockchain technology is a noteworthy technological advancement in forex trading. By improving trade settlement's efficiency, security, and transparency, blockchain—the decentralized, immutable ledger that powers cryptocurrencies like Bitcoin—has the potential to completely transform the forex trading industry. Trader-to-trader transactions can be carried out directly, without the need for middlemen like banks and clearinghouses, by utilizing blockchain-based platforms. Additionally, real-time transaction tracking and verification made possible by blockchain technology lowers the possibility of fraud and error. Furthermore, trade execution and settlement may be automated using blockchain-based smart contracts, which simplifies procedures and lowers operating expenses for market players.

Furthermore, developments in predictive modeling and data analytics are giving traders a better understanding of market dynamics and trends. Traders can examine enormous volumes of market data to find trends, correlations, and anomalies that could affect currency prices by using big data analytics and machine learning algorithms. Traders can make more strategic and well-informed decisions thanks to this data-driven approach, which eventually improves trading profitability and performance. Trading professionals can foresee trends and seize new opportunities by using predictive modeling techniques like sentiment analysis and time series analysis, which offer insightful information about future market movements.

Moreover, traders can now execute trades with the least amount of latency from anywhere in the globe thanks to the development of cloud computing and high-speed internet connectivity, which has democratized access to forex markets. With the robust features and functionality of cloud-based trading platforms, traders can manage their portfolios, execute trades, and access real-time market data from any internet-enabled device. Furthermore, without having to invest in expensive hardware or infrastructure, cloud computing allows traders to take advantage of strong analytical tools and algorithms. Due to the democratization of access to the forex markets, investors and retail traders now have more options, leveling the playing field and encouraging increased competition and innovation within the sector.

In summary, technical advancements are causing a great deal of change in the forex trading industry and providing traders with new tools and perspectives to help them deal with the intricacies of the currency markets. These developments have the power to completely change how traders interact with the forex markets. They range from blockchain technology and sophisticated analytics to algorithmic trading and artificial intelligence. In the fast-paced, constantly-changing world of foreign exchange trading, traders can enhance their competitive advantage, maximize their trading performance, and seize new opportunities by utilizing technology. Consequently, the future of forex trading is inextricably linked to the unrelenting advancement of technology, opening up new avenues for opportunity and possibilities in the international currency markets.

Impact of Global Economic Events

Economic events have a profound effect on the complex network of global financial markets, affecting asset prices, market sentiment, and investment strategies. Numerous factors can cause market volatility and uncertainty, impacting traders and investors globally. These factors range from central bank policy decisions and geopolitical tensions to economic indicators and natural disasters. Participants hoping to negotiate the intricacies of financial markets and seize new opportunities must comprehend the ramifications of these global economic events.

Monetary policy announcements from central banks frequently cause substantial movements in the currency, bond, and equity markets, exerting considerable influence over the world's financial markets. Market expectations and investor sentiment can be influenced by policymakers' outlook on economic growth, inflation, and monetary conditions, which can be communicated through interest rate decisions, quantitative easing programs, and forward guidance statements. In order to take advantage of expected market reactions, traders constantly watch central bank statements and communications for hints about the future course of policy. As a result, they modify their positions and strategies accordingly. The significance of keeping an eye on central bank activities is further highlighted by the fact that interventions by central banks, such as currency interventions or unconventional monetary policies, can have a significant impact on exchange rates and the prices of financial assets.

Furthermore, geopolitical developments have the potential to have a significant impact on the world's financial markets by bringing volatility and uncertainty that affect all asset classes. Investor risk aversion can be sparked by geopolitical tensions, wars, and diplomatic disputes. This can result in a flight to safety into conventional safe-haven assets like gold, the Swiss franc, and US Treasury bonds. On the other hand, progress in diplomatic or geopolitical negotiations can increase optimism and appetite for risk, which can lead to rallies in riskier assets like stocks and emerging market currencies. Traders need to be aware of geopolitical developments and how they might affect asset prices and market sentiment. In addition, geopolitical developments have the potential to upend international supply chains and influence the cost of commodities like natural gas, oil, and agricultural products, which increases their influence on financial markets.

Economic indicators also play a crucial role as gauges of the state and performance of the economy, offering information on employment, inflation, growth, and consumer spending trends. Important economic releases like the GDP, job reports, inflation data, and retail sales figures have the power to move markets because they cause traders to reevaluate their expectations and positions in response to fresh information. Economic indicators are also frequently updated and revised, which complicates the interpretation and analysis of the market. To navigate market volatility and take advantage of trading opportunities, traders need to be highly knowledgeable about economic fundamentals and have the ability to accurately interpret data releases. Economic data from powerful economies like the US, the Eurozone, China, and Japan also have a big impact on the direction of monetary policy and the outlook for global growth, which makes them extremely important in the world's financial markets.

Furthermore, environmental catastrophes and natural disasters can have a significant impact on international financial markets by upsetting supply chains, influencing commodity prices, and resulting in liabilities and insurance claims. The market may experience volatility and uncertainty as investors evaluate the effects of natural disasters like hurricanes, earthquakes, floods, and pandemics on corporate earnings, economic growth, and central bank policy decisions. Traders need to be flexible and quick to react to new developments, modifying their plans and risk-reduction procedures to minimize losses and take advantage of new opportunities in impacted markets. Events linked to climate change, such as severe weather and sea level rise, also present systemic risks to economies and financial markets, emphasizing the necessity of risk management and sustainable investing strategies.

Furthermore, new opportunities and challenges for traders and investors are being brought about by technological advancements and innovations, which are changing the global financial markets. The emergence of algorithmic trading, artificial intelligence, and high-frequency trading has revolutionized the way markets function. These days, automated trading systems analyze enormous volumes of data in real-time and execute trades at breakneck speeds. These technological advancements provide new opportunities for profit maximization and risk mitigation, but they also bring with them drawbacks like heightened market fragmentation, liquidity problems, and possible systemic risks. Traders need to adjust to these developments and take advantage of technology, but they also need to be aware of the risks that come with the quick development of new technologies. Additionally, by improving the efficiency, security, and transparency of trade settlement and clearing procedures, technological advancements like blockchain and distributed ledger technology (DLT) have the potential to completely transform the financial markets.

In summary, central bank policy decisions, geopolitical tensions, economic indicators, natural disasters, and technological advancements all have a significant influence on market dynamics and investor sentiment. These events have a profound and wide-ranging impact on financial markets. A thorough understanding of these factors and how they affect asset prices and market volatility is essential for traders and investors. Traders can successfully negotiate the intricacies of the world's financial markets and seize new opportunities for risk management and profit generation by being knowledgeable, alert, and flexible in their strategy development. As a result, continuing advancements in technology, geopolitics, and the global economy will influence the direction of financial markets going forward, offering opportunities as well as challenges to players in the market everywhere.

Emerging Currency Markets

As the world's financial landscape continues to change, emerging currency markets have become more prominent and dynamic players. For traders and investors looking for diversification and growth, these markets, which include currencies from developing and transitioning economies, present special opportunities as well as difficulties. Emerging currency markets, which are influenced by variables like economic growth, political stability, and global market dynamics, offer a wide range of investment opportunities. These include frontier markets in Asia and Africa as well as the economies of Brazil, Russia, India, China, and South Africa.

Emerging currency markets are characterized by their inherent volatility and uncertainty, which can be attributed to various factors including economic imbalances, geopolitical tensions, and currency crises. These markets have a high potential return, but there is also a high risk involved, such as capital flight, currency devaluation, and sovereign default. To reduce possible losses, traders and investors need to carefully consider the risk-return profile of investments in emerging currencies and use effective risk management techniques. Furthermore, there can be large variations in the liquidity of emerging currency markets; certain currencies have limited trading volumes and wide bid-ask spreads. Because of this, traders need to be patient and cautious when placing bets in these markets, especially when volatility is high.

Furthermore, emerging currency markets frequently act as gauges of investor confidence and global risk sentiment because of their close ties to larger economic and geopolitical developments. Prospects for economic growth, political stability, and fiscal restraint all have a significant impact on how emerging market currencies perform; positive developments promote appreciation while negative developments cause depreciation. Furthermore, as the Asian financial crisis of 1997 and the global financial crisis of 2008 demonstrate, emerging currency markets are vulnerable to outside shocks and cascading effects. In addition to keeping an eye on geopolitical events and macroeconomic indicators that could have an impact on emerging market currencies, traders and investors need to be alert to these systemic risks.

Furthermore, because of structural reforms, demographic trends, and technological advancements, emerging currency markets present special investment opportunities. Growing middle-class consumption, internet penetration, and rapid urbanization are driving economic growth and innovation in emerging markets, opening doors for investors to profit from consumer-driven industries like technology, healthcare, and e-commerce. Furthermore, structural changes that promote market liberalization, better governance, and increased transparency are drawing in foreign capital and enhancing emerging economies' chances for long-term growth. These trends can be used by traders and investors to find emerging currency investment opportunities that have good risk-return profiles and room for growth.

Furthermore, the global financial system is integrating emerging currency markets more and more, and cross-border capital flows have a big impact on how currencies are valued and how the markets behave. The currencies of emerging markets are significantly impacted by foreign direct investment, portfolio investments, and international trade flows. Short-term fluctuations in exchange rates are frequently caused by changes in capital flows. Furthermore, central banks actively participate in emerging market exchanges in order to control inflation, stabilize exchange rates, and promote economic expansion. In order to take advantage of new opportunities and reduce risks, traders need to stay aware of these factors and their potential effects on the currencies of emerging markets. They should also modify their trading strategies as necessary.

In addition, new developments in technology are changing the structure of emerging currency markets and opening up new trading and investment opportunities. With trades being completed at blazingly fast speeds and volumes, the emergence of electronic trading platforms, algorithmic trading, and high-frequency trading has completely changed the way that currencies are bought and sold. Furthermore, the development of financial technology, or fintech, is opening up access to developing markets for currencies, making it easier and more efficient for investors and retail traders to trade currencies. Furthermore, by lowering transaction costs and boosting financial inclusion, blockchain technology has the potential to completely transform international payments and remittances in developing nations.

To sum up, emerging currency markets are vibrant and becoming a bigger part of the world financial scene. They present traders and investors with both opportunities and challenges. Global market dynamics, political stability, economic growth, and currency volatility and liquidity from developing and transitioning economies are some of the factors that shape these markets. In order to take advantage of new opportunities and reduce risks, traders and investors need to carefully evaluate the risk-return profile of emerging currency investments, keep an eye on macroeconomic indicators and geopolitical developments, and modify their trading strategies. Because of this, emerging currency markets have the potential to become more and more important in world finance, stimulating innovation, expansion, and diversification for all players in the market.

Regulatory Changes and Their Effects

In the ever-changing world of regulations, adjustments frequently represent significant turning points that influence both businesses and industries. Laws, rules, and policies governing a variety of industries, from finance to healthcare and beyond, can be changed through regulatory changes. Numerous factors, such as emerging risks, changing societal norms, economic conditions, and technological advancements, are driving these modifications. Businesses must comprehend the effects of regulatory changes in order to comply, adapt, and prosper in the dynamic regulatory environment.

The financial sector is one prominent area where regulatory changes have significant effects. In the aftermath of the 2008 global financial crisis, regulatory bodies across the globe enacted comprehensive reforms aimed at augmenting stability and alleviating systemic risks. Stronger capital requirements, more transparency, and oversight mechanisms for financial institutions were introduced by policies like the US Dodd-Frank Act and the global Basel III Accord. Although the goal of these modifications was to increase the financial system's resilience and rebuild public confidence, they also presented banks and other financial institutions with new operational and compliance requirements. Institutions' profitability and competitive positioning were impacted by the significant resources they had to devote to improving risk management frameworks, restructuring their operations, and guaranteeing regulatory compliance.

Similar to this, laws governing healthcare are frequently updated to take into account new developments in technology, public health issues, and changing patient needs. For example, major changes were brought about by the Affordable Care Act (ACA) implementation in the United States, which included increased insurance coverage, quality improvement initiatives, and payment reforms. Healthcare providers, insurers, and pharmaceutical companies faced difficulties in implementing the Affordable Care Act (ACA), despite its goals of increasing access to healthcare and reducing costs. Adherence to value-based reimbursement models and the adoption of electronic health records were two ACA requirements that necessitated significant infrastructural and operational changes. Furthermore, industry stakeholders frequently experience volatility and disruptions to their strategic planning due to regulatory uncertainty surrounding changes in healthcare policy.

Recent years have seen a rise in the prominence of regulatory changes in the field of technology and data privacy. Global governments have implemented strict laws like the California Consumer Privacy Act (CCPA) and the General Data Protection Regulation (GDPR) of the European Union due to the spread of digital technologies and worries about data security and privacy. In an effort to strengthen people's right to privacy and prevent data breaches, these regulations place stringent requirements on organizations regarding the gathering, handling, and archiving of personal data. Nonetheless, substantial investments in cybersecurity, data governance, and regulatory compliance frameworks are required to ensure compliance with these regulations. Because non-compliance can lead to significant fines, harm to one's reputation, and a decline in customer confidence, proactive regulatory compliance efforts are crucial.

Furthermore, regulatory changes frequently affect broader economic dynamics and societal trends in addition to having a significant impact on particular industries. Environmental regulations, for example, have an impact on businesses in a variety of sectors, including manufacturing, transportation, and energy, with the goal of promoting sustainable practices and lowering carbon emissions. In addition to requiring companies to invest in renewable energy sources, adopt sustainable business practices, and adopt cleaner technologies, these regulations also seek to address urgent environmental issues like pollution and climate change. The shift towards a more environmentally friendly economy offers prospects for advancement and expansion; however, it also presents obstacles for sectors that depend on conventional, high-carbon methods.

In addition, the need for unified regulatory frameworks to promote international investment and trade has grown as a result of globalization. In order to promote regulatory coherence, lower trade barriers, and harmonize standards and regulations across jurisdictions, international organizations and regulatory bodies are essential. Multinational firms may face difficulties complying with regulations due to disparities in national regulatory frameworks and priorities. Stakeholders must continue to communicate, work together, and make concessions in order to harmonize regulations while taking into account different national interests and regulatory cultures.

To sum up, regulatory changes play a crucial role in reshaping industries, influencing strategic choices, and affecting the interests of stakeholders in the ever-changing business landscape. Although the goals of regulatory reforms are to improve consumer protections, address urgent societal issues, and foster economic stability, they also present difficulties for businesses in terms of compliance, operational modifications, and strategic planning. Proactive engagement, investment in compliance capabilities, and a keen understanding of the implications of the regulatory environment are necessary for adapting to regulatory changes. Through proactive approach to compliance, anticipatory planning, and staying up-to-date with regulatory developments, businesses can effectively navigate complex regulatory environments and seize new opportunities as they arise.

CONCLUSION

A thorough manual for new and seasoned traders alike, "Forex Trading Frontier: Navigating Currency Markets for Profit" provides comprehensive guidance in the ever-changing realm of foreign exchange trading. Readers will travel through the complexities of currency markets throughout the book, learning advanced strategies, essential concepts, and useful advice for success.

One thing becomes very clear as the last pages of this insightful book are turned: forex trading is more than just forecasting currency fluctuations; it's also about developing your risk management skills, keeping up with world economic trends, and utilizing cutting-edge trading tools and technologies. The book skillfully leads readers through the territory of sentiment, technical, and fundamental analysis, enabling them to take advantage of profitable opportunities in the constantly changing forex market and make well-informed trading decisions.

Furthermore, "Forex Trading Frontier" emphasizes the value of perseverance, discipline, and ongoing learning in order to achieve long-term success, going beyond the technical aspects of trading. Whether readers' goals are to increase their income, become financially independent, or just learn more about currency markets, this book gives them the information and abilities they need to confidently and skillfully negotiate the forex trading frontier.

"Forex Trading Frontier: Navigating Currency Markets for Profit" is, all things considered, a priceless tool for anyone looking to get started in or advance their career in the exciting field of forex trading. Insightful analysis, useful advice, and real-world case studies are combined in this

book to show readers how to become profitable in one of
the financial markets' most exciting and lucrative sectors.

Thank you for buying and reading/ listening to our book. If you found this book useful/ helpful please take a few minutes and leave a review on the platform where you purchased our book. Your feedback matters greatly to us.